COLLECTING
Teddy Bears

Collecting
Teddy
Bears

SALLY TAYLOR

TODTRI

This book was designed and produced by Todtri Productions Limited
P.O. Box 572, New York, NY 10116-0572 FAX: (212) 279-1241

Printed and bound in Singapore

ISBN 1-57717-004-0

Author: Sally Taylor

Publisher: Robert M. Tod
Designer and Art Director: Ron Pickless
Editor: Nicolas Wright
Typeset and DTP: Blanc Verso/UK

Contents

Introduction

There is one companion from our nursery days who travels easily into adulthood with us – often more easily than we do! – keeping our childhood and adolescent secrets while ready to listen to more, silently offering comfort whenever we need it, and guarding our friendship with a loyalty that never wavers. It is, of course, the teddy bear. Since this little chap appeared at the beginning of the twentieth century, people have cuddled it for comfort, kept it with them for luck, used it as a confidant and a role model, and given it as a symbol of love. For almost a century the teddy bear has been the most enduring of soft toys, often ravaged by affection. Now, it is finding a new place in the hearts and homes of many – as the basis of a treasured collection.

People who collect teddy bears have a special name, arctophiles, and their hobby is known as arctophily. Both terms derive from the Greek words, *arctos* (meaning bear) and *philos* (meaning love). How appropriate, for there can be few other objects that are collected and cared for with such affection, each teddy individually treasured as the character it is.

Those in the caring professions – doctors, nurses, psychotherapists and so on – have long recognized the therapeutic powers of teddy bears. Besides bringing the comfort associated with hugging, teddy bears have been used to teach nurturing skills and to help people come to terms with emotional disturbances buried from earlier times. The police use them as they try gently to break through to a traumatized child or adult; many charitable organizations adopt the teddy bear as their symbol, for we all identify with its tender qualities. There is even an international humanitarian organization – Good Bears of the World – founded in America by a broadcaster and journalist, Jim Ownby, which supplies teddy bears to sick children as well as to those in need, be they elderly, infirm or disturbed, the world over. It was greatly aided by the involvement of a famous arctophile, Colonel Bob Henderson, who recognized just how much a teddy bear can mean. Colonel Henderson's favourite bear, Teddy Girl, with these caring associations, reached the record price for a teddy bear when it was sold at auction in 1994 – an amazing £110,000 (approximately $166,000).

In this book we look at the story of teddy bears as they have marched through this century and into the sale-rooms of today's auction houses. We consider why it is that man has been fascinated with bears through the ages and how the teddy bear developed. We look at the modern phenomena of limited edition and artist teddy bears and the ephemera that has always surrounded teddies. We look, too, at a few basic thoughts about collecting these furry friends.

Peter Bull, one of the best known of arctophiles on both sides of the Atlantic, wrote a book called *A Hug of Teddy Bears*, thus putting a new, and most appropriate collective noun into circulation. The most commonly used term of endearment between couples is "bear" – can there be anyone, anywhere in the world, who does not feel better for the unconditional friendship of a teddy bear?

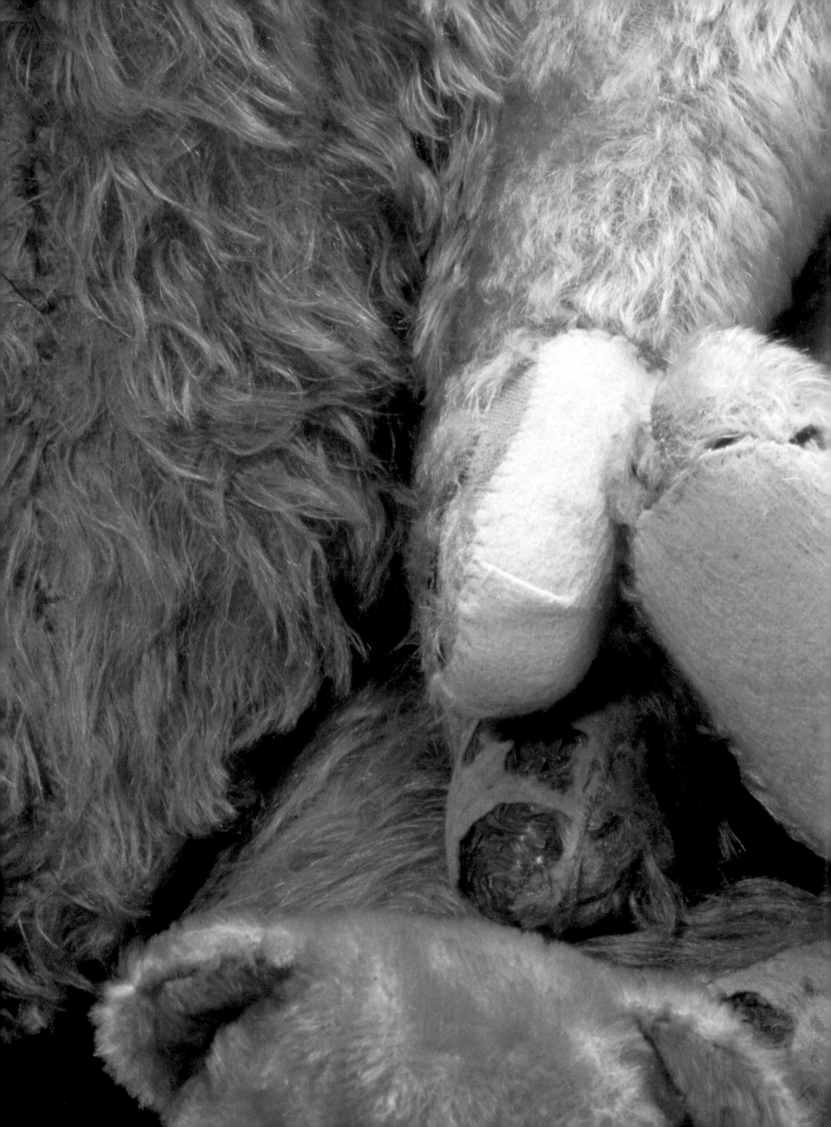

Chapter One
Why Teddy Bears?

Why Teddy Bears?

Opposite: Looking playful and submissive, a young grizzly enjoys the sunshine, although the open mouth lends an air of menace.

Below: It was a cub of either the American black bear or the American Grizzly bear that was the inspiration for the original 'teddy bear'.

I f the teddy bear is the most widespread and popular of all soft toys or models – love and fascination for it often lasting way beyond child-hood – the fact remains that it was originally modelled on one of the largest and reputedly most savage of wild carnivores. Why should it be that the bear, a beast that has inspired fear into man and has been the object of his hunting expeditions from the very earliest of times, should end up as this, the most enduring of all animal models?

The truth is that in addition to hunting the bear and killing it to use for food and warm clothing, humans have through the centuries actually revered this furry animal and used it for their own entertainment. Cave paintings in which bears are the most frequently depicted animal have been discovered dating from the fourth and fifth centuries, but images of bears dating from 25,000 years before that have been found scratched on cave walls. Later, almost wherever bears roamed, models made of clay or primitive-ly shaped bears carved from pieces of wood have been found.

Proof of our early fascination with bears, this artistic expression also points to something deeper. In prehistoric times figurine models would often be made to indicate some kind of worship rather than to serve as a toy or decora-tion. The bear's appeal lay not just in it magnifi-cence and strength, but also in the fact that it could rise up and walk on its hind legs, like a human, while using its arms in apparently human fashion. Many early myths and stories tell of bears that take on human form by day, donning bearskins at night when they go out to hunt. In one of these a young girl lost in the wood is rescued by two young men who take her back to their den on the mountain side, where everyone is wearing bearskins. The young girl stays as a bear's wife and in turn gives birth

Below: Two scenes from the favorite nursery tale, *Goldilocks and the Three Bears*. The bears are given human clothing and also human reactions in the story; notice the displeasure portrayed on the faces of Mummy and Daddy bear as they realise someone has eaten Baby bear's porridge, and Baby bear's tears when he finds his chair has been broken.

Opposite: Christened 'Gilbert', this rare Steiff 'Bär Dolly' teddy bear was made around 1913 and sold at London's Christie's in 1994. The bears were specially produced for the 1913 American election; Steiff made red, white and blue bears in three sizes for this occasion.

to twin boys, half-human and half-bear.

In much early mythology, the bear was depicted as a goddess, displaying the quintessence of motherhood. The fact that bears in the northern hemisphere disappeared through the cold and dark part of the year and reappeared, often with one or two young cubs by their sides as the earth began to thaw out and regenerate in the spring, suggested three things to early man: that these were animals perfectly in tune with cosmic forces; that they were somehow able to regenerate – to be "reborn" each spring; and that the appearance of cubs when the female had been alone in her den was a link with the virgin birth. Any one of these would have been sufficient to turn the bear into some sort of deity – the three together must have been overwhelmingly compelling.

Quite early in our history, the bear was elevated to a place in the northern hemisphere's night sky, identified as the astral constellations, Ursa Major and Ursa Minor – Great Bear and Little Bear. The interesting thing is not so much that these incorporate the brightest star in the sky, the Pole

Star, by which early sailors navigated when they were lost at sea – giving thanks to the bear as well as to their "lucky stars" – but that in widely differing parts of the world peoples as diverse as the ancient Greeks, Inuits, Hindus and the Ostyaks of the area we know as western Siberia, among others, placed the bears in the heavens, independently of one another.

The Inuit explanation for the heavenly *ursus* concerns a woman who lived with some bears for a while and, on returning to her human husband, betrayed their existence. With their all-seeing intelligence, one bear is despatched to kill the woman, which he does, but he is then set upon by the husband's dogs. In a blinding light both bear and dogs rise to heaven where the dogs pursue the bear to this day. Perhaps this story contains a moral for modern teddy bear lovers – betray a bear at your peril. Arctophiles are, indeed,

The Presidential Bear made by Canterbury Bears, of Canterbury, Kent, UK. This company, makers of exclusive teddy bears, were commissioned to make two bears for the inauguration of President Clinton and the Vice-President, Al Gore. The Presidential bear was made in specially woven silk and wears the Presidential seal.

vehement on the seriousness of breaking a promise to a teddy bear!

The hunting of bears in early times would seem to be at odds with mankind's reverence for the animal. When hunting wild animals was a matter of survival rather than a so-called "sport", however, the rituals that surrounded the hunting of bears preserved, even enhanced, the bear's sacredness. The bear had to be killed in a particular manner, the carcass dismembered and disembowelled in a certain way, and ritual ceremonies had to be performed thereafter. And this appears to have been the case whether the bear was killed in North America, across northern Europe and Eurasia or in Japan. It is interesting that these are the places where the teddy bear is held in especially high esteem today.

As humans became more knowledgeable, apparently more "civilized" and yet perhaps less in touch with nature, so the bear began to be an object of entertainment. Sadly, now it began to be degraded rather than revered. Early Romans found amusement in fights between bears and gladiators, while dancing bears, bears performing in the circus and bear-baiting were viewed as spectacles and sport over much of Europe. Travelling menageries featuring performing bears were a common sight, down the eastern seaboard of the United States of America from the middle of the eighteenth century. Early models of bears, before the true birth of the teddy bear, tended to be modelled on dancing bears or bears on all fours, frequently mounted on wheels, so that they could be towed along in the manner often seen in the streets. No lover of bears – teddies or otherwise – could countenance the treatment of bears or the way in which they were trained throughout these times.

Even then, however, not everybody viewed the bear simply as an animal that could be exploited. That it was still regarded by many as having a noble significance can be seen by its appearance in numerous coats-of-arms, ranging from those of towns and cities to those of individual families. Some people believe that the capital of Switzerland, Berne, takes its name directly from the German word for bear, *Bär*, and it is true that the animal is depicted in the city's coat-of-arms. For hundreds of years bears were raised in the bear pits that lie beneath the city. In Britain, Beaumont, Chamberlain, Craddock, Galbraith, Phillips and Vincents are just some of the families whose coats-of-arms feature a bear. Numbers of words associated with, or derived from, the word bear entered the language – bury, burial and bier all derive from the Indo-European root, *bher*, from which bear also comes; to bear (a child) has a direct link; Bruno, Bjorn and Bernard are all names that translate directly as bear in different languages; and the term berserk, which originally referred to a Norse warrior who fought with frenzied fury, derives from a warrior gaining extra courage by clothing himself with a bear pelt.

From the stories of mythology to literature was but a small step and one that the bear took in its stride. It is without doubt the animal – humankind apart – that has most dominated literature, making a very early appearance. From the nurturing mother-figure of the early mythological stories, the bear soon takes on a more aggressive warrior-like status. The early English poem, *Beowulf*, is considered to be the first major poem in a European vernacular language, and the hero's name has been translated as bee-wolf or bear. Ultimately the hero's strength is passed on to King Arthur, whose name in Latin, Arcturus, means bear. The banner of King Arthur shows a bear – an indication of that strength

In many early stories, the bear is characterized as being particularly chivalrous – a link to its heraldic connections. In others it shows up as something of a moral figure, featuring in romantic tales with young ladies; providing they treat it with courtesy and kindness, it will ultimately turn into the handsome prince of their dreams. The Beast in the fairy tale, *Beauty and the Beast*, is often depicted as a bear.

Russia, a land much associated with the bear, has numerous fairy tales featuring bears; the best known was Mischka, which by the eighteenth century had appeared also as a wooden model and even a toy that could climb up and down ladders. In 1898 Tsar Nicholas II is said to have presented a fun version to guests, although this bore little resemblance to

Above: Once much-loved teddy bears find a home as mascots on the front of this truck.

Below: Two fine examples of carved wooden bears made in the 1850s.

15

Opposite: A clockwork drinking bear, probably made in the 1890s.

the teddy bear as we know it. In the 1980 Olympic Games held in Moscow, Mischka appeared as the Games' mascot.

Among the best known of all fairy tales is that of *Goldilocks and the Three Bears*, first published in the 1830s and still told to children the world over today. In this the bears are organized into a human family of a Daddy bear, Mummy bear and Baby bear, alias Goldilocks, who cries like a human child. The story gives Mummy and Daddy bear recognizable parental roles and illustrations generally depict all the bears standing on their hind legs and dressed in human clothes according to their gender.

A mid-nineteenth century American story tells of "The Big Bear of Arkansaw" – a hunter who tells how "the greatest bear was killed, that ever lived, none excepted". President Clinton, who came from Arkansas, had in his possession one of only two existing "Presidential" teddy bears especially made by a small, family-run teddy bear manufacturer in Canterbury, England. The teddy bear's links with the President of the United States go way back to the beginning of this century, however; they are deep and of the utmost significance in the history of the teddy bear.

Right: A flat tin plate model of a performing bear and its owner from around 1800.

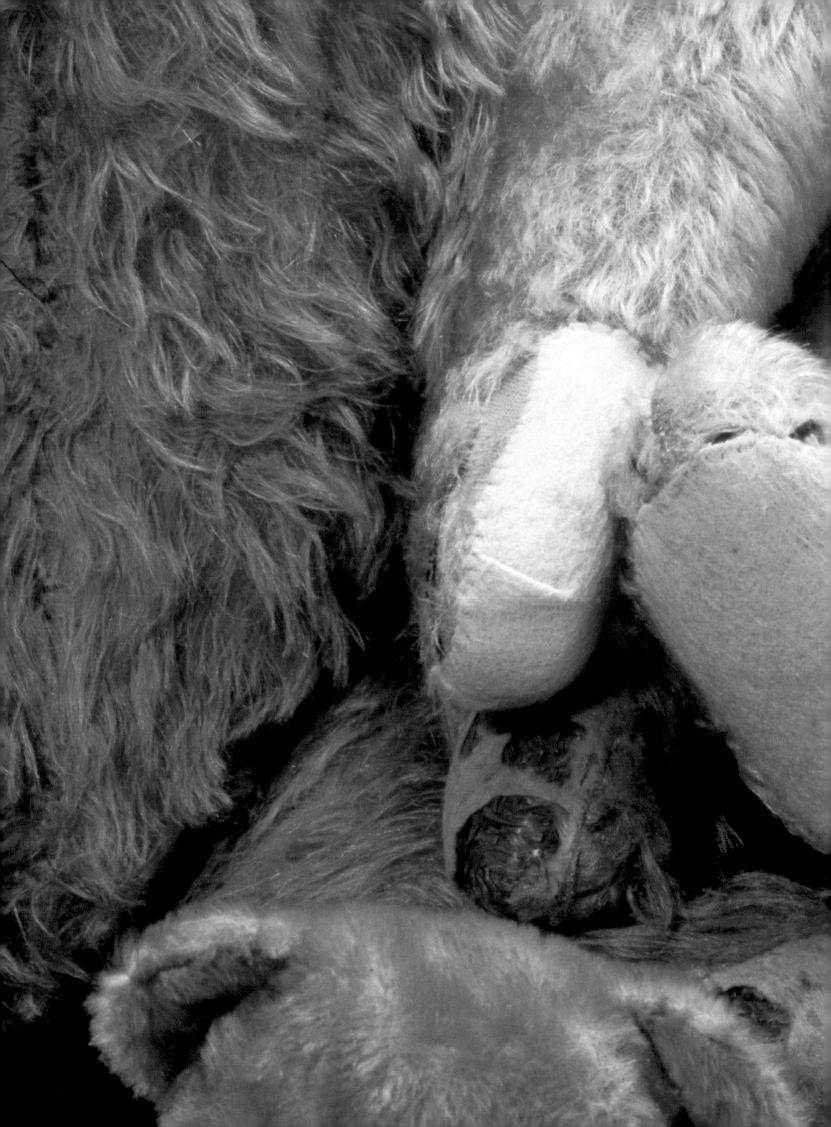

Chapter Two

Teddy Bear Beginnings

Teddy Bear Beginnings

The story of the birth of the teddy bear is well known; most experts and arctophiles trace it to November 1902, when the 26th President of the United States of America, Theodore Roosevelt, known to his friends as Teddy, celebrated the settlement of a border dispute in the southern part of the country by taking time off to go bear hunting. The story goes that all attempts to drive a bear in front of the President's gun failed; ultimately a bear cub was captured and tied to a tree at which point the President was called. A big game-hunter and sportsman, as well, incidentally, as a conservationist, the President refused to shoot the hapless animal.

Photography being only in its infancy at this time, news events were generally portrayed in the newspapers by illustrators. Travelling with the President on this trip was a cartoonist and newspaper artist, Clifford K. Berryman, who drew the incident, which then duly appeared in the *Washington Post* with the headline, "Drawing the Line at Mississippi".

Although there are other versions of what exactly happened during this hunting trip, sufficient numbers of eye witnesses have confirmed this report for most people to adopt it as the true story. What apparently happened next is that Rose Michtom, the wife of an on-the-ball Russian immi-

Steiff bears are always instantly recognizable by their button-in-the-ear trademark.

grant who ran a stationery, confectionery and toy shop in Brooklyn, made a soft, jointed bear modelling it on Berryman's cartoon figure. It is said that the Michtoms wrote to the White House asking the President's permission to call it "Teddy's bear", and the story runs that Roosevelt granted this, while modestly saying that he could not see how this would help with sales – perhaps one of history's great modest understatements! No record of this correspondence has ever been traced, but distance has lent the tale authenticity as well as enchantment. From that time on, the teddy bear became inextricably linked with President Roosevelt.

Less than two years later, in 1904, Roosevelt was faced with an election,

and it is from this time that the first "promotional" teddies date, for a bear that closely resembled the one portrayed in Berryman's cartoons became an important part of the President's election campaign. Ranging in size from 6 to 12 inches (15–30cm), little googly-eyed (sideways-glancing) teddies were made and thrown from the Presidential train as it toured the country. Roosevelt supporters sported a teddy bear hanging from a disc pinned to their coat lapels, which read: "Won't you be my teddy?" Rival campaigners tried to spread stories that Roosevelt had little time for teddy tears, but the public, in turn, had little time for the stories, so completely had the little plush teddy bears captured their imagination.

Above: This large Bruin on wheels was manufactured by Steiff in 1910.

Overleaf: A slightly tattered early Steiff bear.

Left: President Theodore Roosevelt, the man generally held to be responsible for the teddy bear. An active outdoor military man as well as a politician, he is seen here astride his horse in the uniform of the volunteer cavalry regiment he raised, known as the 'Rough Riders'.

Overleaf: Teddy bears from the Edwardian era strike various poses in their nursery setting. The bear on the left wearing an eye bandage may have been one to have accompanied a soldier to the trenches of the First World War, or he may wear his bandage as a comfort to an injured child.

Many people attribute at least some of the responsibility for Roosevelt's re-election in 1905 to the teddy bear. Interestingly, Roosevelt did not stand for re-election in 1908, and in the following year he travelled to British East Africa, where he collected specimens for the Smithsonian Institute in Washington. This Institute has recently ordered its own bear to be made by Canterbury Bears. He sits resplendent with a key to the Smithsonian Castle around his neck.

While the teddy bear was experiencing birth and popularity in the United States, it was also being "born" on the other side of the Atlantic, in Germany. There can be no doubt that its origins were quite separate here, not influenced, at least initially, by the Michtom's teddy bear or the story of the President. Just as those early people in different parts of the world set the bear in the sky independently of one another, so the teddy bear was experiencing dual, quite separate origins.

Above: Quick to realise the appeal of the little cuddly toy to which he had given his name, President Roosevelt used teddy bears as campaign mascots, as well, apparently, as table decorations at his inauguration ball in 1905.

The story in Germany begins with a family by the name of Steiff, now synonymous with teddy bears. Margarete Steiff was born in July 1847, and by the time she was eighteen months old she was suffering the ravages of polio – a disease that was to leave her bereft of the use of her legs and with only partial use of her right arm and hand. Her parents added sewing

Above: A very fine example of a modern day artist bear.

Below: Margarete Steiff, at work in the factory in Giengen, Germany.

lessons to her daily schooling, and she went on to become a talented seamstress as well as an astute businesswoman. She initially set herself up in the felt-working business, but when this fabric became unfashionable for ladies' clothes, she developed a sideline hobby of producing felt toys. Her first venture was an elephant, which could be a child's toy or a pincushion gift for an adult. It was her brother, Fritz, who recognized the commercial potential of these toys, but he convinced his sister only when he sold a sackful at a market and returned with orders for more.

Other soft animal toys were added to the range, including, in 1892, a bear on all fours, mounted on wheels. The company was clearly successful as toy manufacturers, so much so, that five of Fritz Steiff's sons joined the busi-

Above: Steiff have always been a family concern. It was Margarete's brother, Fritz, who first convinced her of the market for the soft toys she used to make as a hobby. Here she is seen at the factory with her sister.

Right: His auction tag tied around his middle, this 1926 Steiff 'Dual' mohair teddy bear, made in around 1926, awaits his fate at an auction at Christie's, London. His dark brown mohair fur is tipped with cream and he has eyes of brown and black glass.

Opposite: The Presidential Bear made by Canterbury Bears, of Canterbury, Kent, UK. This company, makers of exclusive teddy bears, were commissioned to make two bears for the inauguration of President Clinton and the Vice-President, Al Gore.

ness. One was Richard, who in his spare time, would go to the zoo and sketch the captive bears, cubs in particular. A gifted designer, in 1902 he created a new model bear, which, while undoubtedly resembling a real bear, was designed along the lines of a jointed doll. It was made of long-haired plush fabric, it had long, movable limbs and a stout body, given a fairly soft filling, and its long snout shaven. Richard's design, known as Petz, used shoe buttons as eyes and replaced the sealing wax nose of the earlier wheel-mounted bears with stitching. The result was a soft toy instead of the much less yielding, all-fours bear or the definitely uncuddly mechanical bears that had so far been the bear representatives on the toy market.

These bears were shipped to New York in February 1903, and the scepticism of Richard's aunt, Margarete, seemed well-founded when they by and large failed to make the leap from the shelves of

New York shops to the nurseries of American families. Notwithstanding this initial failure, Richard Steiff took his bears to the Leipzig Toy Fair the following month, where, probably to his own amazement, he received an order for 3,000 from an American, Hermann Berg, who had been a buyer for some years for the then world-famous toy importers George Borgfeldt & Co. Some experts claim that so great was the influence of this company on the toy industry that had this order not been placed, the teddy bear story might have taken a very different course.

There is no doubt that these two sources, the Michtoms, later to become the Ideal Novelty & Toy Co., of Brooklyn, New York, and the Steiffs, of Giengen, Germany, were the producers of the first teddy bears, and both can claim its earliest origins. Britain will occasionally put in a bid · for the origin of the name, teddy bear, although it has to be said it does not stand up very strongly against the American claim and in itself is pretty half-hearted. Edward VII, king from 1901 to 1910, the period when the teddy bear was originating, bore the nickname, Teddy, and was further known to spend time at the zoo, particularly observing the koala bears (which are not, of course, members of the bear family at all). An obvious tongue-in-cheek attempt to give this somewhat tenuous link a little more weight is contained in the spreading of a hopelessly unreliable story about a nightwear salesman arriving to sell his products at Buckingham Palace. He is said to have been dismissed by the queen, who exclaimed, "We prefer our Teddy bare"!

Where soft toy animals had most frequently been made using real fur, Richard Steiff used the fabric that is still probably the most widely used in teddy-bear making today – mohair plush. This luxurious fabric, which is now available in a range of finishes, is woven from the fleece of the angora goat. Steiff's early teddies, with their long limbs, pointed muzzles and humped backs, tended to be more bear-like than their American counterparts, which were appealing and cuddly from the start. One of the first bears ever made by Richard Steiff was actually grey; known as a 55PB, only a very few were made making it among the rarest, and most valuable, of bears today. Within a year, recognizing that the market requirement was for more instantly "friendly" teddies, Richard Steiff had modified his bears,

Above: Made around 1930 by an English manufacturer, and christened 'Monty', this bear was given to his owner, Peter Hibbert, as a mascot when he went into active service with the Tank Regiment in the Second World War.

Opposite: These bears sit quietly with other Edwardian toys and artifacts. The sampler on the wall gives an indication of the era.

Previous pages: Christmas is a time for teddy bears. This Victorian teddy echoes the theme and era of the artifacts around him.

making the body and limbs less chunky and using a lighter coloured fur. The result was dramatic. By the end of 1904 the Steiff company had sold some 12,000 bears, and Margarete Steiff had been awarded two Gold Medals and the Grand Prix award for her industry and efforts in the toy world.

The first bear Steiff produced in 1903 was referred to as the Bar 55PB and, like its successor, the Bar 35PB, the limbs were made to move by the introduction of cardboard disc joints, attached to one another by strong cord. When it was found that the cord failed to stand up to the strain imposed on it by children's play, it was replaced with wire, but in no time at all, this was considered too dangerous. This led to the introduction for a short time of the famous Steiff rod bear, the Bar 28PB. In this little bear, which had a moulded sealing-wax nose (unique to rod bears), metal rods joined the legs and arms. The upper rod had a vertical extension in the centre that connected the body to the head. The awkward movement brought about by the unyielding rods in these bears made them somewhat unappealing to children, and they were made for only a year. This, however, has greatly increased the appeal of Steiff rod bears to collectors.

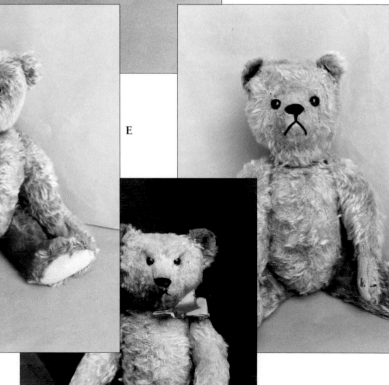

Opposite: A unique blue plush Steiff teddy bear known as 'Elliot'. This was one of six variously colored teddy bears made by Steiff and sent to Harrods Department Store in London in 1908 as samples.

Clockwise from the top: (A) Steiff teddy bear dating from 1909. Still sporting its original eyes and pads and the world famous 'ear button' in its left ear. (B) Thought to be manufactured by Steiff between 1917-20, this mohair teddy bear has button eyes. (C) A very early, cinnamon-coloured Steiff teddy bear, dating from between 1903-1905, remains in excellent condition. (D) This Steiff teddy bear, dating from 1910-1915, has shoe button eyes, and new felt coverings to his paws and feet. (E) Of unknown German origin, this teddy bear is thought to date from 1910. It shows a few signs of age, but all the original materials are intact.

A

B

E

C

D

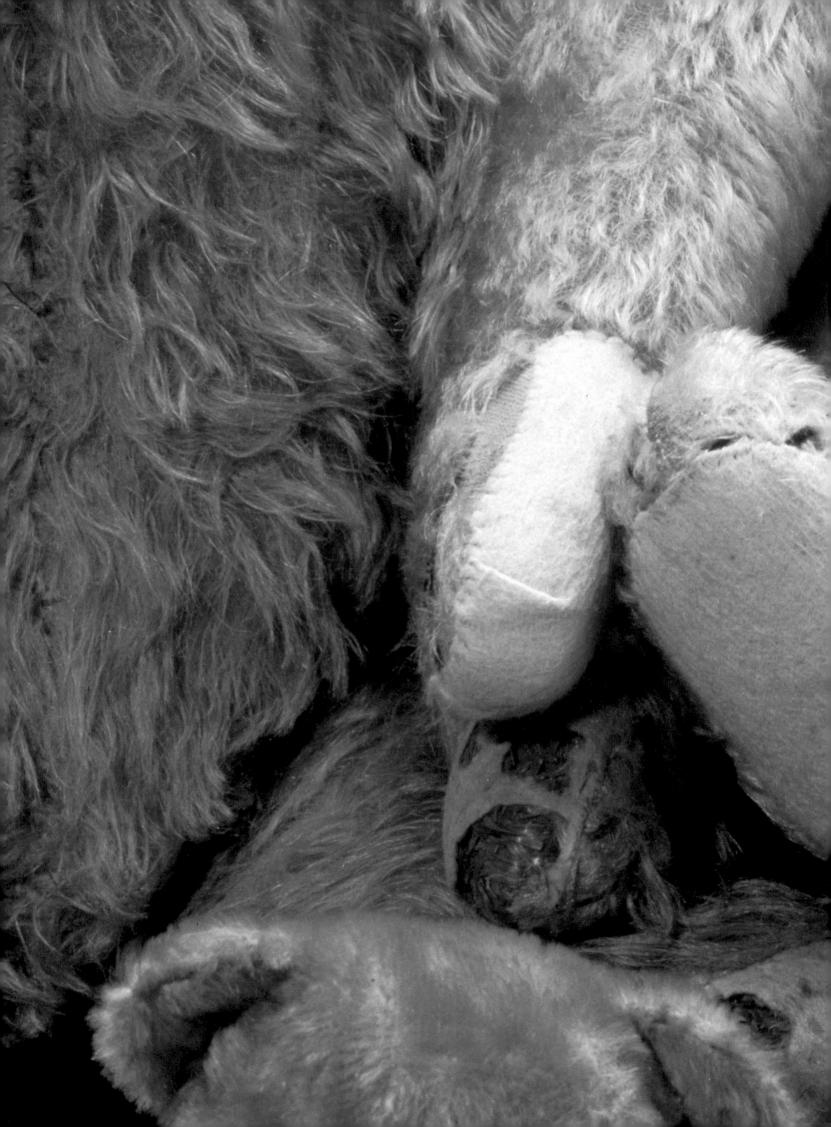

Chapter Three

Boom Bear Years

Boom Bear Years

Opposite: This is a group of hand-made knitted bears from the Second World War. Servicemen carried such bears with them for luck.

Below: Examples of an old and a young Steiff bear.

O nce teddy bears had arrived, everyone, it seemed, wanted them. Right from the beginning they captured the imagination of adults as well as children, and owning a teddy bear, whether you were a girl or a boy, a child or a grown-up, seemed to be acceptable. Inevitably, as the popularity of these little furry fellows was universally recognized, individuals and companies began to jump on the bandwagon, and cheap imitations of the early teddy bears began to appear all over the place.

Germany

Steiff, which has always been the "Rolls-Royce" manufacturer of teddy bears, sought to protect itself from inferior, poorly made copies. The company produced and patented a trademark and logo – a metal button that was riveted to the ear of every bear that left the factory. This, the famous *Knopf im Ohr* (button in ear), initially featured an elephant, representing those first felt toys made by Margarete Steiff; this was superseded by a blank button, and finally, in 1905, a button with the word Steiff on it was used. To this day, Steiff bears carry this trademark, and the company has protected it fiercely over the years, generally taking legal action against any other company that sought to attach identifying buttons in the ears of their teddy bears or even used the word "button". The absence of a button in the ear of an old teddy bear, incidentally, does not necessarily indicate that it is not a Steiff, for many of these were

Two bears enjoying a drive in the famous 1950s Austin pedal car.

removed or simply fell off after years of loving abuse. Old teddies with the button intact are treasured by collectors.

The first teddy bears produced by Steiff, particularly the rod bears, tended to be quite stiff and somewhat uncuddly, in spite of their mohair coats and Richard's early efforts. In 1905, striving towards greater "cuddliness", Richard Steiff introduced a range of bears known as Barle – which translates as "someone dear" – or the PAB range. Until this time the teddy bears were stuffed with a filling of wood wool, called excelsior, which made them really quite heavy and gave a particularly hard finish. Barle bears were filled with a mixture of excelsior and kapok – the downy covering from the seedpods of this tropical tree – which made the bear lighter and softer. The rods were done away with, and instead the limbs were attached to the body with cardboard discs, anchored now with a metal pin, which allowed them to move more freely. It seems that these bears were made in

After Chad Valley had taken over a company called Peacock & Co - manufacturers of printed wooden blocks - they introduced the Peacock range of bears, of which this is a fine example. This bear was sold at an auction at Bonham's in March 1995.

Above: A Merrythought Dutch teddy bear from the late 1930s sports a wide-legged pair of trousers.

Right: Artist bears come in all sizes and colors, dressed and undressed. Is this a case of always the bridesmaid, never the bride?

Below: This cuddly fellow, with his big head and ears and uncertain expression, is reminiscent of Merrythought's Cheeky range.

various sizes from 6 to 32 inches (17–80cm) – the measurement being taken to the top of the bear's head when it is in a seated position.

In the year 1907, a year known at Steiff as the "Golden Year of the Teddy", the company sold nearly one million bears. However, as it introduced more and more to its range, not all the bears were greeted with open arms. One, a black bear with a blunt muzzle and a much less pronounced back hump, proved sufficiently unpopular that only a fairly small number were produced compared with the other bears of the time. This, of course, makes it a much sought after bear by modern collectors, who also greatly favour the miniature bears Steiff was also producing. The eyes of early ones, intended as mascots for World War I servicemen, were placed

high up on the head so that they could look out of their owners' pockets.

Steiff also made dressed bears from this early era. "Bare" bears were popular at this time, made specially for "home" dressing, their wardrobes limited only by the imagination of the maker. Richard's bother, Hugo, skilled in engineering, developed a range of acrobatic bears that tumbled, climbed and swung in a frame.

News of the popularity of the teddy bear, with its significant export potential, soon reached other toy manufacturers in Germany. One was a toy-maker called Johann Hermann, who made a range of little wooden toys that sold well locally. His three children, who helped him in his workshop, seized the initiative and began making teddy bears just at the outset

The entire wedding group. In these artist bears, it is the clothes, rather than different expressions, that give the bears their status and character.

A

B

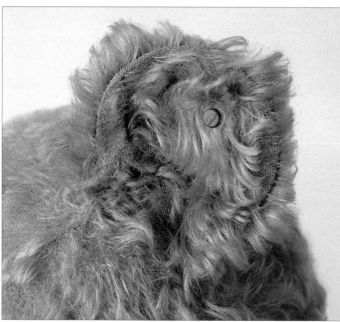

C

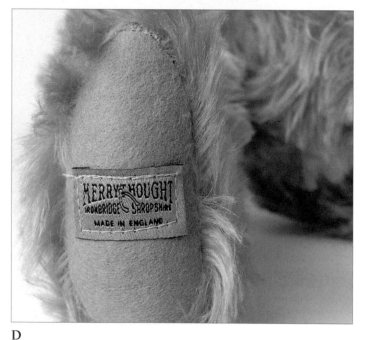

D

(A) The Steiff ear button was always accompanied by the embroidered 'knopf im ohr' tag.

(B) Many teddy bear companies copied the famous Steiff ear button, like this one from the English manufacturers, Chad Valley.

(C) Steiff's ear button, the most famous of them all.

(D) The trademark from one of Britain's most successful teddy bear makers, Merrythought.

of World War I. Although when war broke out the workers had to make ammunition baskets by day, they continued the manufacture of teddy bears by night. These early bears closely resemble contemporary Steiff bears, and because at this time they sported only a tie-on paper tag, which almost always failed to endure, it can be difficult to distinguish between the Hermann and Steiff bears from this period. Often, however, the fur on the muzzles of the Hermann teddy bears is different from the fur on the rest of their bodies.

The name of Hermann is one of the most important in teddy bear manufacture to this day. All three of Johann's children continued to make teddy bears after World War I, and eventually different companies bearing the name Hermann, all associated with top quality teddy bears, came into exis-

Right: British manufacturers, HG Stone & Co Ltd, produced the Chiltern range of 'Hugmee' bears for more than 50 years, beginning in the early 1920s. Initially made from beautifully colored and excellent quality mohair, some were fitted with squeakers, others incorporated a clockwork musical mechanism. This example lives at the Teddy Melrose Museum in Scotland.

Far right: Another enduringly popular range of teddy bears, was the Cheeky range by Merrythought, first produced in the late 1950s. The bears were characterized by the large, somewhat droopy ears set low on the sides of the head, each one incorporating a bell. This bear dates from the 1950s.

Previous page: This rare black teddy bear was manufactured by Steiff around 1910-12 when they made a small batch for the British market. In fact most of these bears had red felt backed eyes, not present in this bear.

tence. They underwent various changes, both of name and location, following the disruptions in Germany through the early decades of the twentieth century, but today successor companies include Gebrüder Hermann GmbH & Co. KG and Hermann-Spielwaren GmbH. These are still basically family firms, run or owned by descendants of Johann Hermann.

Another famous German name associated with teddy bears from this era was that of Gebrüder Bing (known as Bing Werke from 1920) of Nuremberg. This company began its life making domestic tinware, but began to produce a range of extremely popular tin toys, including fine trains. When teddy bears became all the rage, Bing began making them, too, modelling the early ones on the successful Steiff bears. Bing's first teddy bears even had a button in the ear, something that Steiff was quick to oppose in the courts, taking legal action to ban them in 1909. The button was replaced with an arrow-shaped tag and finally a button under the arm; this is usually referred to as a stud because Steiff had claimed the sole right to the use of the word button.

Many of Bing's tin toys featured clockwork actions, and the company soon began designing bears that incorporated mechanisms of various kinds. Before long there were Bing bears that walked, skated, kicked a ball or did somersaults, either on their own or with their arms suspended on framework swings, in a manner similar to the Steiff acrobatic bears. While most companies were making bears in various shades of brown, Bing also made bears in a range of more unusual colours. At one time among the world's biggest toy manufacturers, Bing went out of business in 1932 during the worldwide depression, and the company's early bears are fetching high prices in today's auction houses.

United States

In the United States, the home of the teddy bear – by name, at least – companies mushroomed in an attempt to jump on the teddy bear wagon. Many tried to claim that their goods were of the same high quality as the German bears, but generally they were not. When all is said and done, however, a teddy bear is a teddy bear, and inferior quality in no way effects their love-ability, just their durability. The Michtom's Ideal Toy and Novelty Co. was in full production and was joined in 1906 by the Aetna Toy Animal Co., which produced a range of bears in seven sizes. These could almost be said to be the first "artist bears" – at least, they were advertised as "artist-designed".

Just as German manufacturers tended to model their bears on the successful Steiff ones, American bears from this era all have a similarity to one another. They tend to have triangular-shaped faces with broad foreheads and long muzzles, while the rounded ears are placed high and wide on their heads. Their bodies are moderately long and generally have a less pronounced hump than the German bears. Arms and legs are both quite long and thin. Aetna added an identifying mark to its bears – an oval with the word "Aetna" inside stamped in ink on the left foot. Inevitably, this has tended to fade over the years.

Another company to appear at about this time in the United States was the Bruin Manufacturing Co. of New York, which again produced bears that were identifiable as being of American design. They were quite similar to Aetna bears, although perhaps with a rather more appealing expression. The company's trademark, BMC, stitched in gold thread on a black label, was attached to the pad of the left foot.

Like countless others, sadly neither of these companies lasted for long, but another that was to be far more enduring and that is one of the top names in the USA today is the Gund Manufacturing Co., which actually dates from the end of the nineteenth century. This company claims to be America's oldest soft toy manufacturer, and was founded in 1898. It apparently began to make teddy bears in 1906, producing a small range, although these have not been clearly identified.

Britain

The teddy bear was just as popular in Britain as in Germany and the United States. The first examples to be seen were apparently imports from Steiff, but British companies soon began manufacturing for themselves. Among the first to introduce bears was Dean's Rag Book Co., which began by selling printed

Above: With noticeably small ears and short arms, this 14in (35cm) tall bear is of American manufacture and dates from the 1920s.

Right: Both dating from the 1950s, these golden mohair bears were manufactured by Steiff. Both have had to have some surgery, the one on the left needing a replacement leg!

cut-out cloth patterns of bears very early in the teddy bear boom. Teddy bear fronts in two halves, a back and two feet pads were printed on cotton with instructions for cutting, sewing and stuffing. Advertised as being made for "children who wear their food and eat their clothes", the bears were known for their "indestructibility, washability and hygienic merit", and one of the company's earliest trademarks showed two dogs tearing at one but failing to pull it apart. Dean's went on to manufacture its own teddy bears from about 1915, beginning with one known as Kuddlemee.

The first mohair plush British bear to rival the quality of its American and German cousins was probably made by the company J.K. Farnell & Co., which is said to have produced a bear in 1908. In the absence of specific trademarks, it has proved hard to identify with certainty not only these, but also many of the other British bears that were made by companies that quite quickly came and went in this period. What is known, however, is that the teddy bear was enormously popular in the years leading up to World War I. London stores featured them in their windows, and from this time many shops had teddy bears made specially for them. It became fashionable to own them again, among all ages and classes of society, and they were even quickly adopted as "fashion accessories" and

carried by society ladies. As the war approached, it was both fashionable and patriotic to dress bears in uniform. Nannies the country over would spend their spare time stitching a reproduction uniform of the father of the house for the teddy bears belonging to his offspring. Those from Scottish regiments, for example, would sport the relevant tartan kilt, and where a sailor was joining a particular ship, the teddy bear left behind might have the name of it on a hat made specially for him.

In addition, teddy bears went off to fight the wars with the young men who were drafted into service. Countless stories are attached to teddy bears that were returned to grieving parents after their owners were killed in action. Several of these have found their way into sales at leading auction houses, and their stories told and often backed up with old photographs of them with their owners. One, an English bear from the 1930s called Monty, dressed in the army uniform of the Tank Corps, accompanied his owner, one Peter Hibbert, to war, but was sadly to return home without him. Together with family photographs that helped to verify his story, Monty proved that bears with this sort of history are extremely collectible when he made more than three times his catalogue price at a teddy bear sale in December 1995.

A bear dating from 1930-1940, of unknown origin, shows signs of previous wear. Its pink paws are a recent restoration.

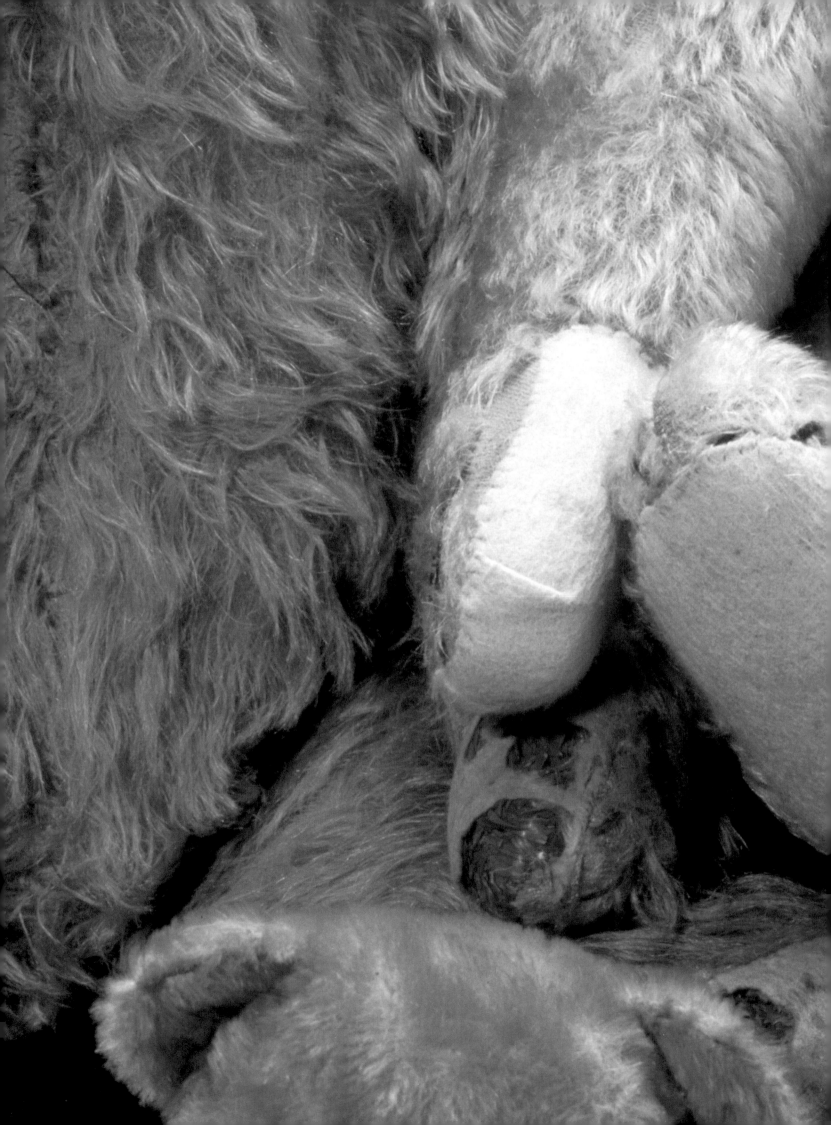

Chapter Four
Teddy Bear Slump

Teddy Bear Slump

Opposite: A blue-eyed, white plush teddy sports lederhosen trousers and a neckerchief. This is a modern artist bear.

Below: A blue Merrythought Cheeky teddy bear dating from the 1950s looks as if he has been much loved over the years. Note the contrasting colored muzzle.

Ever since the teddy bear first made its appearance at the beginning of the 1900s, its popularity has been so apparently assured that it has experienced remarkably little in the way of slumps in sales at any time in its history. The German and British markets were inevitably affected during World War I, when factories were called on to concentrate on making goods for the war effort, and in the years following the hostilities, many European countries imposed a ban on German imports, producing, among other things, their own teddy bears.

Steiff's factory had been given over to making munitions and airplane parts during the war, and it took the company a while to re-establish its position as the leading manufacturer of teddy bears that it had always been. Richard Steiff visited the USA after the war and apparently wrote back that Steiff bears appeared "colorless, sober and insipid" in comparison with the American toys he saw. This was in 1925. A bear Steiff made in 1926 and thought possibly to be a prototype for the Petsy range that was marketed in ten sizes in 1927, was one of the first bears to reach such an outstanding price at auction that it hit the news in a big way. In 1989 it sold for an amazing £55,000 (approximately $83,000) – a record price that remained unbeaten until 1994.

Perhaps also in response to Richard Steiff's comments, in 1926 Steiff produced the "teddy clown"; this bear came in various sizes and colors and sported a neck ruff and pierrot hat. In the 1930s the company's "circus" bear had snap joints and a neck mechanism. Its rarity makes it much prized, and another from the 1930s, the "teddy baby" range, some of which had open mouths and were said to be modeled on a young bear cub, is a great favourite with today's collectors.

The Hermann empire re-emerged as Johann's children married and began to go their separate ways. One son, Max Hermann, married the daughter of a doll manufacturer and they started the company that was originally known simply as Max Hermann but that later became Hermann-Spielwaren. In the 1920s the company pro-

Following the Second World War, many manufacturers economized by producing dressed teddy bears, thereby enabling them to make the body of cheaper cloth rather than expensive mohair or other fur. This 1948 Merrythought Print Teddy is an example; its patterned clothes are an integral part of the bear - not removable.

duced a range of ten teddy bears known as the 112, which varied in size from 8 to 27 inches (20–70cm). Produced in varying shades of gold, each bear had a huge silk bow around its neck. It is said that the first thing a girl apprentice joining the company had to learn was how to tie one of these ribbons.

Perhaps it was the difficulties experienced by the leading German manufacturers during and immediately after the war that enabled other companies to flourish. Indeed, new companies were to emerge everywhere, even in Germany. In Britain a surprising number of companies actually began to make teddy bears during the war years, some started by people who found themselves without employment, others because there was a demand for teddy bears that was no longer being satisfied by German imports.

Raising his hand in salute, this 1930s Merrythought teddy bear is in excellent condition. He still has the original button in his ear as well as a label on his right foot.

In America the demand for bears went on, and in the interwar years a lot of novelty bears were produced. Right from the beginning of teddy bear production on both sides of the Atlantic, some bears had been fitted with "growlers". The earliest of these was no more than a scrunched-up piece of oilcloth, which was placed in the bear's tummy and which vibrated with air when it was punched or squeezed. Later, more sophisticated mechanisms were incorporated, but the vogue for novelty bears also saw the production of bears that whistled or played tunes. Some bears were produced with flashing eyes, linked to a battery (these mechanisms did not prove long-lasting), while others had no legs so that they rolled around but never fell over. In the 1930s an American company made a teddy that "ate" food; as a cord at the back of its head was pulled, its mouth opened to receive

A Chad Valley teddy bear has its original label on the right foot but its eyes have been replaced by buttons. It sits with its smaller post First World War companion.

goodies that could be retrieved by unzipping it.

Perhaps the craze for novelty bears prompted the German company Schreyer & Co. to produce and market its range of Shuco bears. Founded in 1912, this company initially made mechanical toys but was soon producing clockwork bears that would walk or kick a ball. In the 1920s it turned its attention to making tiny teddies – the Piccolo range. Only 2 to 3 inches (6–7.5cm) tall, the bears' fur was clipped mohair wrapped around an internal metal frame or armature. Many of these were developed as "handbag companions" – fashion accessories. The bears' heads came off and the bodies split open to reveal a perfume spray, a powder compact or a lipstick container. For gentleman, the tiny teddies concealed a flask for his favourite drink. The bristly mohair of these little bears was often brightly colored, with green, red and lilac featuring along with the more usual gold.

Also in the 1920s Schuco made larger teddy bears, such as the famous and much sought after Yes/No bears, which were also made in a mini-version. These bears would nod or shake their head, the action being brought

An excellent example of a 1950s Shuco bear. Shuco (Schreyer & Co) began manufacture of teddy bears in Germany in 1912 and were particularly known for their range of tiny teddy novelty bears which opened to reveal a perfume atomizer, powder compact, lipstick container or whisky flask.

about by manipulating the tail, which acted as a lever. Made in varying sizes, some of these incorporated a squeaker or musical mechanism. A rare and very beautiful bear in this range is the Bell Hop bear, which was made wearing the uniform of a hotel bell hop – a red pillbox hat and red coat, together with black trousers. This company also made non-mechanical bears.

Another German company made what has become a famous bear from this era – one that is sought after by collectors, but that, when it appeared, found no favor at all. This is a bear known as Peter. It was made in 1925 by a company called Gebrüder Sussenguth, of Neustadt, near Coburg, which had made dolls and other toys since the end of the nineteenth century and apparently included other teddy bears in its range. Peter, however, remains the best known. Clothed in dark brown fur, the bear had a rather frightening face with rolling eyes and an open mouth with bared teeth and a waggling tongue. The label on the box read *Bar wie lebend* ("bear with the most natural-like finish"), but it was in its box that it mainly stayed, for children found it just too frightening. Although rare, Peter

This cheerful looking teddy bear, dating from the 1930s, was made by Chad Valley, one of Britain's most successful toy manufacturers in the first half of the century. He still has the identifying button in his ear; note it is in the right ear, not the left, as with Steiff.

bears tend to be in mint condition simply because they were never played with. They are a favorite with many teddy bear collectors.

During World War I and immediately thereafter several American firms ceased to trade, many people apparently favoring imported bears. Ideal and Gund continued to manufacture bears, however, and a company that was to make quite a mark on the American teddy bear scene was the Knickerbocker Toy Co. Inc. Founded in New York, this company took its name from the nickname for New Yorkers, derived from the baggy trousers of many of the original Dutch settlers. Knickerbocker had begun to produce toys in the middle of the nineteenth century, but did not produce its first teddy bears until the 1920s. The bears tended to have rather large, wide heads, which were somewhat flat-topped, and blunt muzzles. The central chest seam of each bear had a label with the company's horseshoe

This Merrythought bear, 'Bedtime Bertie', was made exclusively for the Cotswold Teddy Bear Museum. Bearing the typical cheeky face, he is a copy of a bear made by Merrythought in the 1970s.

logo and the words, "Knickerbocker Toy Co. – New York" stitched into it.

Knickerbocker's most famous bear is probably its version of Smokey, but a nice story concerns one of its teddies from the 1920s, a dark brown bear. It became famously known as the "fertility bear", when its owner gave it to her daughter who was having trouble conceiving a child, telling her to put it at the foot of the bed. The story goes that within four years the daughter had had three children and later passed the bear on to one of her daughters who was experiencing the same difficulty. The bear is said to have worked similar magic!

Probably the country to see the greatest amount of new teddy bear activity during these years was Britain, and by the 1920s and 1930s the teddy bear industry was booming, although inevitably the Depression made it hard for small companies to survive. From the beginning, British bears

Three Merrythought Cheeky teddy bears all dating from the 1950s. Their varying conditions tell different stories of love and affection over the years.

have tended to have flatter faces, rather shorter and straighter limbs and less pronounced humps at the tops of the backs (and these soon disappeared altogether) than their German cousins. The woven mohair plush fabric, known as Yorkshire cloth, which had been exported in quantity to Germany before World War I, began to find an extensive market in its homeland.

Among the new companies to become established was the Chad Valley Co. Ltd, which was founded in 1914 but began specializing in soft toys a few years later. Early Chad Valley teddy bears sported a button in the right ear with the word Aerolite written across a cream center. This indicated that the bear was stuffed entirely with kapok, giving a much softer finish than the traditional wood wool. Other companies to produce these softer bears were W.J. Terry, founded in 1913, which produced Ahsolight teddies, and the Teddy Toy Company, which was founded in 1916 and produced the Softanlite range.

Chad Valley remained a remarkably successful company, producing a number of bears in this period and continually adding more teddies to

This careworn, somewhat threadbare bear was made by Merrythought in the 1930s. He turns side-on to the camera to reveal the identifying button placed on his back.

Overleaf: Among the most famous of all 'mascot' bears, 'Mr Whoppit' was owned by Donald Campbell, the one-time holder of the World land and water speed records. This little bear, made by Merrythought in 1956, accompanied Donald Campbell on numbers of his record-making attempts, including the final one on Lake Coniston, where Campbell lost his life. Mr Whoppit came to the surface of the water shortly after the crash.

its range as it took over other toy companies. One of these companies was Peacock & Co., which Chad Valley took over in the early 1930s, and shortly after the acquisition, Chad Valley brought out a new Peacock range of bears, this word being incorporated into the label, together with a peacock motif. In 1938 it was awarded the Royal Warrant of Appointment as "Toymakers to Her Majesty the Queen" (now Queen Elizabeth, the Queen Mother) and was said to be the world's leading toy manufacturers of this time.

Another of Britain's best known teddy bear manufacturers was Merrythought, which is still a leader in the field. The company began to

Teddy bears help to celebrate all occasions. Here, Father and Mother Christmas are set to bring a little festive cheer to any yuletide event.

produce toys in the 1930s, although it had been founded just after World War I as a mohair mill. When it began to find it difficult to compete with the synthetic fibres that were becoming increasingly popular, the Merrythought Company was established to make soft toys that would use the mohair plush. Early Merrythought teddy bears, which had always been rather round and cuddly, were similar to those made by Chad Valley, and, in fact, the two companies' factories were not far from one another and one of Merrythought's first directors had worked for Chad Valley.

The name Merrythought is taken from an ancient English word meaning the wishbone of a bird – the teddies being a "wish come true" – and the symbol has always been part of the company's trademark. Originally it was shown on a celluloid-covered button that was stitched into the left ear; later this was moved to the back of the bear. Merrythought teddies also had a label of black lettering on a yellow background sewn to one or other of the feet. Merrythought's Bingie range (of seated bears based on a bear cub or made with cloth bodies and limbs designed to be dressed) and Magnet or M range appeared at this time and are widely sought after now.

Dean's continued to produce teddy bears throughout this time, as did J.K. Farnell, which was marketing bears with the Alpha label. Renowned as being of a particularly high quality, Farnell bears had hump backs, long muzzles and a distinctive central seam down the stomachs. The label bearing the name Alpha was stitched to a foot pad. In the 1920s, the company produced the remarkable Yeti bear in response to a news item of the day; this funny looking furry chap had no ears!

In 1920 Harry Stone, who had been with Farnell, joined up with the Chiltern Toy Works and together they became the company, H.G. Stone & Co. Soon renowned as producers of quality teddy bears, the company maintained its good reputation right up to the time it was taken over by Chad Valley in the late 1960s.

Chiltern Toy Works was already producing teddy bears when Harry Stone joined the company – one with googly eyes dates from around 1915 – and it kept the name Chiltern for its teddy bears, the factory being situated in the Chiltern hills in southern England. Its most famous teddies from this time are probably the Hugmee bears, which are sometimes said to be among the finest quality "character" British bears ever produced. They remained popular right up to the time of the Chad Valley takeover. Made from very good quality mohair and filled largely with kapok, the bears were designed to be particularly cuddly, as the name suggests. Early bears often had a squeaker, while later ones were fitted with clockwork musical mechanisms.

France, Holland, Switzerland and Australia all went into the manufacture of teddy bears at this time. Early French bears seem to have been modeled on the dancing bears popular throughout the French countryside in earlier centuries. Dancing bears were popularly known as Martin, the name given to the hero of a comic strip bear in the nineteenth century. Some of the early French toy bears incorporated a mechanism that enabled them to dance and among them was one called *L'ours Martin*. French companies known for post-World War I production of teddy bears were M. Pintel Fils & Cie., FADAP and Thiennot.

Opposite: Merrythought's 'Punkinhead' bear, with its striking contrastingly coloured, long-haired topknot, was originally made exclusively for Eaton's department store in Toronto. First appearing in 1949, it was a precursor to the Cheeky range.

Below: A cuddly 11in (28cm) tall bear made by the successful German manufacturer, Hermann, in the 1940s. By this time there were two manufacturers of teddy bears in Germany bearing this name, Gebruder Hermann, which began in 1911, and Hermann-Spielwaren GmbH which was founded in 1920 under the name of Max Hermann & Sohn.

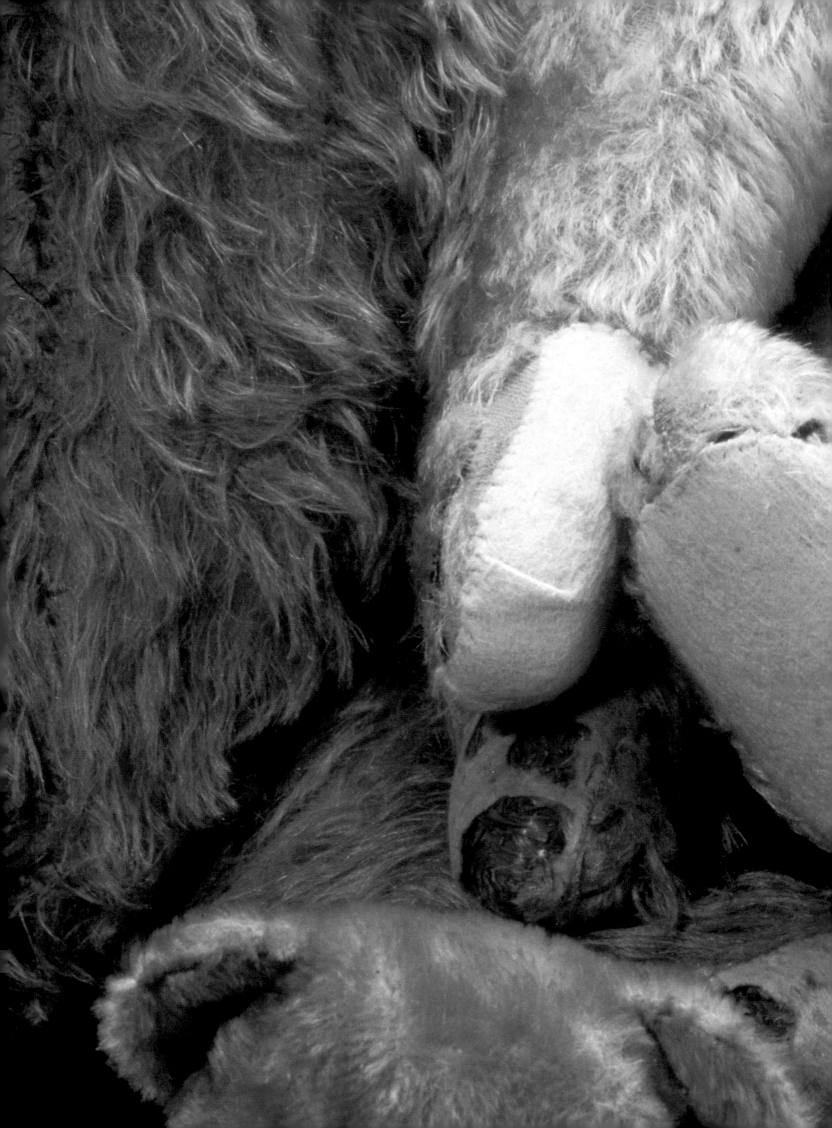

Chapter Five
The Bear Revived

The Bear Revived

World War II may have seen a fall in the numbers of teddy bears on the market as materials were in short supply and factories were called on to manufacture items for the war effort, but there was certainly no less a demand for these furry companions. What greater comfort to a child being evacuated away from the dangers of bombs to some seemingly far-off part of the country than to tuck a much-loved teddy bear under his or her arm at the start of the unknown journey? Servicemen going off to fight would often take along their childhood bear or one given to them by a loved one in the

A 1939 postcard, sent by a grandfather to his grandson on his birthday.

Left and below: Teddy bears have always been popular with young children. And many of them carried their favorites on into adulthood.

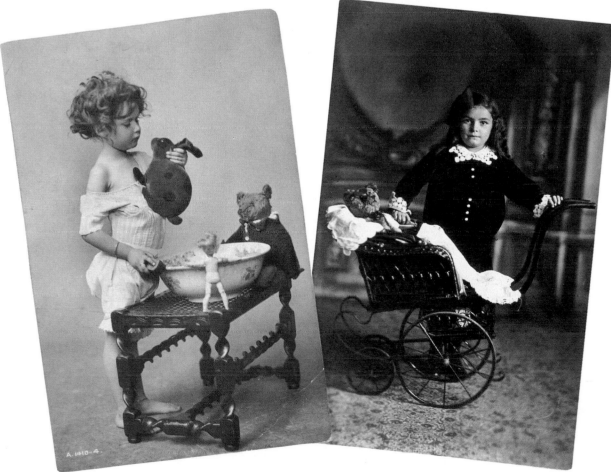

A group of modern day bears huddle closely together. Note a Paddington bear on the left of the back row, sporting a jaunty striped football jersey. The bear in the centre of the back row has a long muzzle which has been shaved, a feature that is popular among some collectors.

Overleaf left: Old-time nursery favorites remain together as they stare nostalgically back into times gone-by.

Overleaf right: 'Grandfather' from Canterbury Bears, made to celebrate the 15th Anniversary of this very successful family company. Described as an old-fashioned traditional bear with woodstraw filling, he comes with a grandchild bear. The fob watch hanging round his neck has a photograph of founder, John Blackburn, with his grandchildren.

A 1950s teddy bear with a highly prominent growler in his middle. Growlers and squeakers have been incorporated into teddy bears from their earliest times. One of the first types was no more than a bag of scrunched up oilcloth with a reed inside; when the bear's tummy was squeezed or punched, the rush of air in the oilcloth made the reed vibrate.

hope it would act as a talisman. Others would give bears to girlfriends, fiancées and wives as companions, reminders and guardians against the time they returned. The stories of such bears are legion; sadly, many have less-than-happy endings.

The years 1939–45, and even beyond, could reasonably be termed the era of the homemade bear; mothers and aunts knitted teddy bears or made them from any scraps of soft cloth they could find, including scraps of sheepskin and old blankets, often following patterns given in magazines, so that children should not have to go without this essential companion. Teddy bear manufacturers did still produce bears but had to resort to using cheaper materials, cotton plush replacing mohair and a sort of waste from the textile factories known as "sub" often used for stuffing. The felt usually

Left: Fine examples of 'corporate' bears - that is 'house' bears specially commissioned for a company or store. On the left is a bear made by Canterbury Bears for Liberty; the one on the right was made by Merrythought for Burberry. Both bears have fabric associated with these companies on their pads.

used for the pads was replaced by cheaper fabrics, too. Hermann, and possibly other manufacturers, would accept orders to make a single teddy bear, often using fabric sent to them by the anxious client.

The stringent conditions did not come to an end with the war and the teddy bear manufacturers continued to have to find ways to economize to some extent. Many made dressed bears, the clothes being an integral part of the bear – not removable – so that they could use cheaper cloth underneath.

Manufacturers had other problems to contend with as the 1940s passed into the 1950s. Teddy bears had always been quite expensive to make, particularly the jointed bears made with quality cloth. Now the demand was for cheaper toys, and this meant serious competition from the development of manufacturing bases in the Far East, initially in Japan, which was to become a major toy-producing nation, and then (still much in evidence today) China, Korea, Taiwan, Thailand and Indonesia. In addition, Britain and America were imposing more stringent safety standards on the production of soft toys.

A new manufacturer in Britain, Wendy Boston, started in 1946 and set

Left: Harrods Department Store has a long association with teddy bears and each year numbers of manufacturers produce special bears for them. This one is a Harrods Doorman Bear made by Merrythought.

More corporate bears made by Canterbury Bears. From left to right, these were made for Liberty, the famous toy store - Hamleys, and Laura Ashley. Note the Hamleys bear has feet pads of the same plush as the rest of the bear, rather than the more usual contrasting fabric.

Miniature bears are very popular with many collectors. This one was made for Burberry by Merrythought; his fur has been clipped to make it more suitable for such a small bear.

Opposite: This little Merrythought Cheeky bear was made specially for Harrods. Note the Harrods label on his foot and also the characteristic green coloured ribbon round his neck.

Canterbury Bears, founded in 1980, are among the most successful companies in the field of corporate bears. Here is one they made for Laura Ashley.

high standards of safety and hygiene from the outset. Indeed, these teddies were marketed under the reassuring name Playsafe. Synthetic fibres had been developed and refined by this time, and they were popular not just because they could be dyed easily in a wide variety of colors but because they were also washable. Wendy Boston's largely unjointed bears were made in woven-nylon plush, were filled with a foam stuffing and were given a new kind of apparently unbreakable "screw-lock" eyes, and the makers boasted that they were the first machine-washable bears. In the early 1950s this manufacturer also made some conventional jointed mohair teddy bears, which are favorites with collectors today.

Pedigree Soft Toys was another new name in British teddy bears at this time. Actually started in the 1930s, Pedigree was a subsidiary of Lines

Brothers, a large and very successful toy manufacturer, perhaps best known for its Tri-ang trademark. The early Pedigree teddies had rather long heads, although with short muzzles, and shorter limbs than many of the other manufacturers' bears. In the 1950s the bears had characteristic plastic noses and smiling mouths.

The established manufacturers fought to conform to the required standards, while also bringing out something new at prices that could compete in the newly expanding markets. In fact, however, in many instances it was their continued attention to high quality and detail that carried them through. The year 1953 marked the fiftieth anniversary of the first Steiff bear, and the company brought out Jackie bear in three sizes to mark the occasion. Designed to look like a bear cub – and sometimes known as

One of Canterbury Bears' old-timers, in fact now designated the firm's Head Bear, this is 'Flash' - a 15-year-old mascot bear, who is described as a world traveller. His floppy ears and spectacles give him an air of dignity befitting to such a wise and gentle bear.

Another beautiful bear, but one in quite a different style, from Canterbury Bears. This is 'Rodney Bloomfield' - a classic bear made of 100 per cent distressed mohair. He measures 23ins (58.5cm) from head to toe and has long arms and legs as well as very pronounced claws.

Jackie-baby – it was particularly round and cuddly, despite the protruding muzzle. The most noticeably unusual characteristic, however, was a horizontal stitch in pink near the top of the vertically stitched dark brown nose.

Two years before this, Steiff had brought out one of its enduring and popular ranges, the Zotty bears. These chubby chaps were made distinctive by their long-haired mohair coats, shaven muzzles and open mouths, which had a peachy-colored felt lining and a painted tongue. So popular were these teddies that they were quickly copied by other manufacturers. Steiff Zotties, however, generally have fur of a slightly contrasting color on the chests.

In addition to being Steiff's fiftieth anniversary year, 1953 was the year of the coronation of Queen Elizabeth II. Merrythought marked the occasion

This is the bear for the man who has everything. Canterbury Bears' 'Dressing Gown Bear', who made his appearance in 1984, is a camel hair bear with a matching dressing gown. Note the coat-of-arms on the dressing gown; soon after they began production, Canterbury bears were awarded the privilege of adopting the ancient coat-of-arms of the City of Canterbury, dating from the 11th century.

with a coronation bear in patriotic red, white and blue. It was also in this decade Merrythought brought out its Cheeky bears, probably among the company's most enduringly popular teddies ever. These bears, with their downward-looking, characteristically low-set eyes, over-large ears – often incorporating a bell – squashy noses, wide grins and large, wide feet, followed on from a bear known as Punkinhead, which Merrythought made especially for Eaton's Department Store in Toronto, Canada. The bears had striking topknots of long, contrasting colored hair.

In America the teddy bear business was still booming, and although Gund, Ideal Toy and Novelty Co. and Knickerbocker Toy Co. were all still producing bears, the field was becoming increasingly dominated by multi-national, conglomerate companies. An important teddy bear was produced by both Ideal Toy and Knickerbocker in the postwar era – Smokey, the for-

A 'gaggle' of 'Gregorys'! This is the very first bear that Canterbury Bears produced in 1979. Although made in various sizes, they all share the same features and are made of gold English mohair.

est ranger bear, was created for the Cooperative Forest Fire Prevention Campaign to increase public awareness, particularly among children, of the danger of starting forest fires. Ideal made the first Smokey bear in 1953. It had a moulded vinyl head and paws, and children owning one could become Junior Forest Rangers. Smokey was a great success, both as a character – the Smokey Bear Act was passed by Congress in 1952 to prevent the bear being exploited for other campaigns – and as a teddy bear. Versions were still being manufactured up to the mid-1980s and probably beyond.

Right: This shaggy little blue-eyed chap is known by its makers, Canterbury Bears, as 'Louis Poodle', for obvious reasons! It is made completely from sheepskin which is shaved to sculpt the face and feet.

Smokey was, of course, a powerful tool in an advertising or promotional campaign, and bears have long been used in this field. Countless manufacturers of products as diverse as ladies hosiery to wine gums, from corsets to cough mixture, from coffee to petrol, have used the teddy bear as an advertising aid. Leading department stores as well as smaller shops have had their own

A classic teddy bear from Canterbury bears, this one was designed to celebrate the 10th anniversary of the company in 1990. Made of pale brown English wool, he was made in a limited edition of 500.

teddies made. Some of the bears were wholly made in a fabric that was instantly associated with the shop; other bears were produced with just the paws made in an identifiable material; still other bears had the name of the store emblazoned across a foot for all to see as it sat on a chair or table top, bed or mantelpiece. Not only a constant pointer to the source, these teddies all suggest an exclusivity as well. Stores would, and still do, commission special bears from manufacturers to mark notable occasions or anniversaries. In 1986, for example, Harrods, the prestigious London store, brought out a special Christmas teddy bear, and in 1995 it offered customers a boxed set of the ten Christmas bears the store had produced to that date.

And just as teddy bears were given as talismans to soldiers going off to

Opposite: A novelty teddy bear - it is actually a purse as can be seen clearly in the photograph with its original owner. This jaunty little chap dates from around 1918 and is in excellent condition.

Right: Och hye! These special tartan bears, from Canterbury Bears, are made in the tartan of a customer's choice. Pictured her is a McKinnon tartan bear - the maiden name of Maude Blackburn, wife of founder, John.

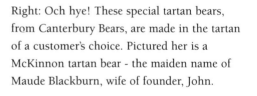

Overleaf: Bears of all ages contemplate their lives together. Top right is a fine example of a Paddington bear, complete with duffle coat, wellington boots and a care label. Below him is a Rupert Bear, who celebrated his 75th anniversary in 1995; he has been given a new scarf to replace the usual checked one.

World Wars I and II, so have they also been widely adopted as mascots by the famous. Amy Johnson, who in 1930 became the first woman to fly solo from Britain to Australia, took a teddy bear with her. Donald Campbell, the British car and speed-boat racer, had a teddy mascot with him when he broke the existing land and water speed records during the 1950s and 1960s. His companion-at-speed was a small, unjointed bear made by Merrythought in 1956 and christened Mr Whoppit. When Donald Campbell made his fatal attempt at the world water speed record on Lake Coniston in England's Lake District in 1967, Mr Whoppit was all that survived the horrendous crash. Thereafter he accompanied Donald Campbell's daughter, Gina, in her speed record-breaking attempts, finally coming up for sale at Christies Christmas teddy bear auction in 1995.

For many decades clubs and associations, especially those associated with sport, as well as organizations from all walks of life have adopted

Teddy bears crop up everywhere! Here one is an important part of the design of a colorful Christmas waistcoat.

teddy bears as their mascots, often dressing them in the appropriate uniform or sports regalia. Teams have no hope of winning matches if they are not accompanied by their bear; brave fire-fighters feel more confident when the station's mascot sits in the fire engine – the power of the teddy bear is ubiquitous!

Many such mascots were simply a bear that had been bought by someone or perhaps produced after being found hidden away at home. In recent years, however, it has become increasingly common to commission the making of a specially required teddy bear. In many ways, this is not new. As we have already noted, department stores have often commissioned their own individual teddy bears. Such orders, however, would be for a number of teddy bears. Now, it is not unusual for just one bear to be commissioned.

Opposite: 'Theodore', a miniature Steiff teddy bear dating from 1948. This bear, a favourite belonging to the English actor and arctophile, Peter Bull, was given to him to celebrate a first night by his friend, Maurice Kaufmann. It reached an amazing £13,000 ($19,500) when it was sold at Christie's 1995 December auction.

Three tiny teddies from Germany dating from the 1950s. Each one holding a baby's bottle, these little fellows have been designed to wear as brooches.

Manufacturers that have survived into the late twentieth century – Steiff, Hermann, Merrythought and Dean's – are all familiar with this phenomenon, and the fact that the old, hand-making skills live on at least to some extent at their factories makes it possible for these companies to produce "one-off" bears. New manufacturers have sprung up that also take on such commissions. One such British company is Canterbury Bears, which was founded in 1980 by John and Maud Blackburn and is still run by them today, although they are now joined by their children to make this a truly family concern. They found themselves in the teddy bear business when John, an artist, was asked at a party to design a teddy bear as a gift for someone's grandmother. The bear was a success, and the company has gone from strength to strength, adding new bears each year as well as designing special bears for shops, museums, hospitals, charities – such as Save the Children – the Walt Disney Company and so on. It has also made special tartan bears using the tartan of an individual's clan.

To some extent the appearance of such specialist manufacturers as Canterbury Bears has coincided with an increasing interest in teddy bears among adult collectors and the seemingly ever-increasing appearance of the teddy bear artist. The term "teddy bear artist" is widely accepted among arctophiles and teddy bear experts, yet it is not easily defined. The "movement" is recognized as beginning in America in the late 1970s, when designers and craftspeople began to make one-off, original bears by hand. Inevitably, more and more people took up their needles and cottons, in Europe as well as America, until today there are literally hundreds of bear artists.

Different people will give different definitions of what makes an artist bear. Originality and quality are among the key criteria, as is the lack of any kind of mass-production. Beyond this, some people feel the artist should be the one that conceives the bear and makes it in its entirety; others feel an artist can be helped by outworkers, who work to the artist's original design to make part of the bear. Everyone agrees that the teddy must have a certain something that makes it special: its character must shine through its face so that the bear is instantly appealing in some way. It is not enough for a bear to be well made, it must, it seems, also convey a message – be it humorous or emotional – just one of the ways of saying "I love you"!

Looking somewhat mournfully into space, this careworn bear was made by Steiff in the 1960s

Perhaps partly in response to the appearance of the artist bears, in the 1980s many of the leading teddy bear manufacturers began to produce limited edition bears as well as replicas of their famous bears from the past. A manufacturer may make a limited edition specifically for the UK or the American market, or it may make one for a particular outlet. An example is a rare red Steiff bear dating originally from 1908. This bear, known as Alfonzo, is particularly special because it came into being through a commission to Steiff from George Mikhailovich, the Grand Duke of Russia, who wanted to give his daughter, Princess Xenia, a teddy bear. Princess Xenia and Alfonzo survived the Russian Revolution, during which her father was assassinated, because they were visiting Britain at the time. Here they both stayed, Princess Xenia ultimately marrying before moving to America; Alfonzo stayed with her until her death. The proprietor of a specialist teddy bear shop, Teddy Bears of Witney, near Oxford, bought Alfonzo at an auction at Christies in May 1989, paying a record price at the time of £12,000 ($18,600). Thereafter Steiff made a replica of Alfonzo, which is available only through this shop near Oxford.

Every year since 1980 Steiff has made one or two replicas of bears of the past, the quantities varying from as few as 750 up to occasionally as many as 16,000, but more usually between 5,000 and 10,000. Other manufacturers – Hermann, Dean's and Merrythought – have followed suit, making replicas of old bears in their range as well as new limited editions. One of Merrythought's replicas, produced in a limited edition in 1992, is of the 1953 coronation bear, again produced in red, white and blue. The company has also produced a replica of Mr Whoppit. Newer manufacturers, such as Canterbury Bears, generally bring out new limited edition bears each year. In 1995, for example, Canterbury Bears produced a bear called "grandfather" to mark the company's fifteenth anniversary. The bear was designed by Maud Blackburn, who describes it as having all the love of the family and the company embodied in it.

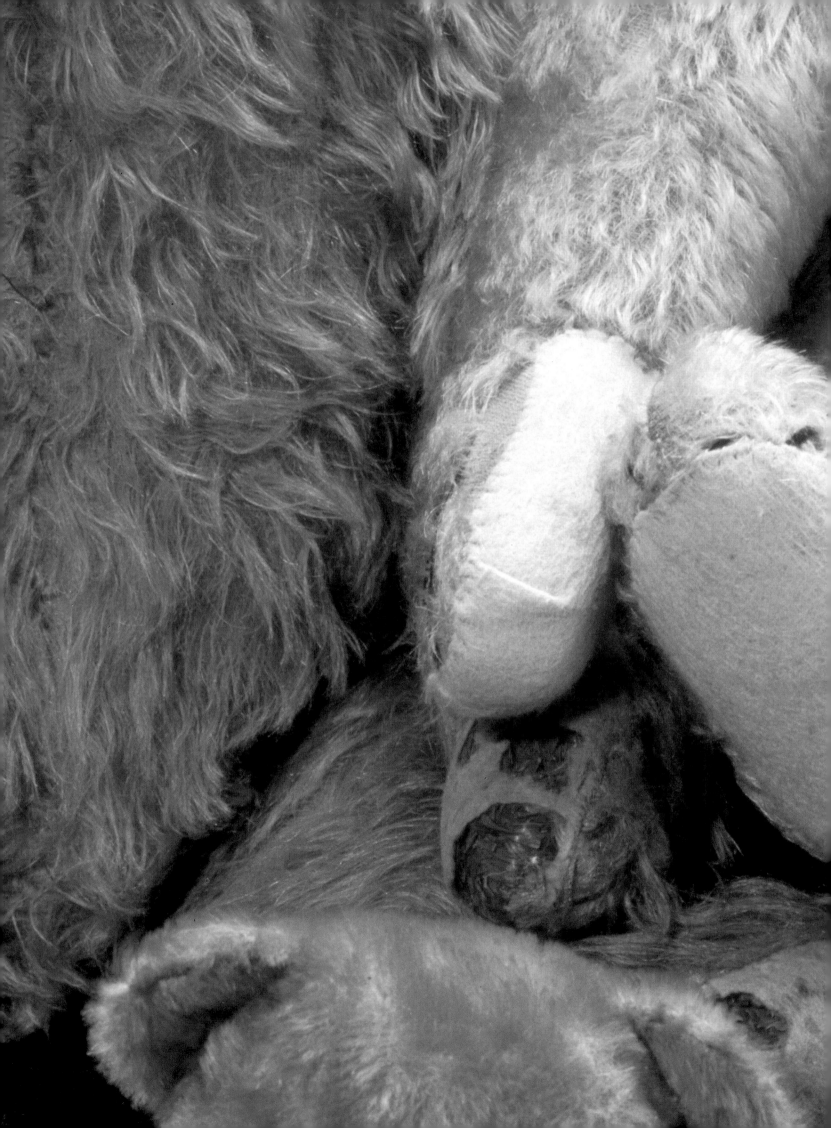

Chapter Six

Media Bears & Bear-obilia

Media Bears & Bear-obilia

We have seen that long before the birth of the teddy bear at the beginning of this century, bears were the heroes, and anti-heroes, of many folk and fairy stories. Pre-twentieth-century illustrations often depicted the bears standing up and using their paws in a human way. They even appeared clothed in some instances – apparent precursors of the teddy bear. With the appearance of the teddy bear toy, however, there followed a host of stories about bears, in which the illustrations were now definitely modelled on teddy bears, and the bears and their adventures veered towards the anthropomorphic. The teddy bear craze, however, extended far beyond the publication of stories and the production of cuddly teddy bears.

Right: Postcards depicting teddy bears have been popular from Edwardian times and form the basis of many collections. They may be cute, humorous or incorporate a timeless message.

Opposite top: On the left an early cheeky postcard! On the right, a French card depicts a tea party from 1913 with a teddy bear playing a central part.

Opposite below: More old postcards showing once more how teddy bears have been constant companions to children through the ages.

BEARLY TIME TO WRITE.

RUN FOR A DOCTOR QUICK! HE'S LOSING ANY AMOUNT OF SAWDUST!

Mary with her little bear behind.

SALON DE 1913 — Mlle Jeanne BEITZ — Société des Artistes Français
Mademoise..e Chrysanthème   Miss Chrysanthemum
Мадемуазель Хризантема

AWANDA in the kitchen   WEDNESDAY

"Let's sit on the lid" said Teddy

GOT A "CIGAWETTE" PICTURE?

"WHEN I'SE SAD AND WEARY,
AND TIRED OF ALL MY TOYS,
I WISH YOU'D COME AND SEE ME,
AND BRING SOME LITTLE BOYS."

One of the earliest teddy bear stories to appear this century, originated, perhaps not surprisingly, in the United States in 1905. It told of the adventures of the Roosevelt Bears, Teddy B. and Teddy G. and was the brainchild of a children's writer, Seymour Eaton. The bears were later to be made as dressed teddy bears by a company in Maryland.

The most famous fictional bears, however, must surely be three separate creations from the pens of British writers. In the order in which they appeared, if not necessarily in their order of fame, they are Rupert Bear, Winnie-the-Pooh and Paddington Bear.

Rupert Bear made his first appearance in 1920 as the very definitely boy hero

Above: In this postcard the bears take on human characteristics .

Opposite: Rupert and Sooty in latex form.

Below: The cover of this early Rupert *annual carries the scribbles of a former owner.*

of a comic strip that was published in the *Daily Express* newspaper. Newspapers of the day tended to have a resident cartoonist. A writer and illustrator called Mary Tourtel, whose husband worked for the *Express*, was chosen to create Rupert for the newspaper. At first Tourtel's illustrations were of a typical teddy bear with a long nose and rounded ears that stuck up either side of his head, but he was soon given a more rounded head and a snubber nose. Rupert was a success from the start. His adventures

often had magical overtones or involved travel, for Tourtel was influenced by classic fairy stories and was an intrepid traveller herself. In 1932 the Rupert League was formed. Children were encouraged to join the League, among whose aims were "to be cheerful" and "to make people happy".

Rupert is having adventures in the *Daily Express* to this day, more than seventy years on. He has survived a number of writers, as well as the often turbulent events of his time. One of the best known of his writers and illustrators was Arthur Bestall, who took over from Mary Tourtel. Bestall was actually the one who depicted him in his now famous red jumper and yellow-and-black-checked trousers and scarf. In Tourtel's time, if Rupert appeared in color, it was wearing a blue jumper and grey scarf and trousers.

Winnie-the-Pooh is probably the world's most famous fictional teddy bear, his adventures having been translated into more than twenty languages, including Latin. He is actually based on a real teddy bear, one bought by Dorothy Milne at Harrods, London, in 1921 for her son, Christopher Robin, on his first birthday. Dorothy's husband, Alan Alexander Milne, started to write stories about the bear, whose original name was Edward Bear, and these were first published in 1924 in an anthology of poetry, *When We were Very Young*. Soon after, it seems, the bear's name was changed to Winnie-the-Pooh – Winnie after an American black bear that was in London Zoo and Pooh, somewhat bizarrely, from

Above: How small can a bear be? A selection of tiny, yet extremely flamboyant, bears. Even the one sitting on the model bear's head is brightly dressed.

Opposite: This bear is sporting a smart red jumper but seems to have lost his trousers!

Entitled 'Sepia Cottage', this feminine little bear poses beneath a rustic bower, the autumn colours of which are reflected in the fabric of her dress and bow. She was made by Britain's Elaine Lonsdale for Companion Bears.

the name of Christopher Robin's favorite swan. However the bear got his name, his adventures published in the subsequent Winnie-the-Pooh books – *Winnie-the-Pooh* (1926) and *The House at Pooh Corner* (1928) – have been staples of childhoods the world over ever since. In the illustrations, drawn by Ernest Shepard, Winnie-the-Pooh is incidentally based on a Steiff bear belonging to Shepard's son, and not Christopher Robin's teddy, which is thought to have been made by J.K. Farnell.

Paddington Bear, the creation of author Michael Bond, is another fictional character to be based on a real teddy bear, one he bought for his wife from Selfridges department store in London in 1956. Paddington was so-called after the London railway station of the same name near which the Bonds lived, and a large Paddington bear has stood on the concourse since the late 1970s. The bear's adventures began when he arrived at the station from "darkest Peru" and began experiencing life with its "quaint customs"

Opposite: The famous Paddington Bear who arrived on Paddington Station from darkest Peru in 1958. In the original drawings he wore a somewhat crumpled and tatty hat, coat and scarf. It was only later he adopted the duffle coat, wellington boots and characteristic hat with the front brim turned up.

Left: Everyone's favourite bear, AA Milne's Winnie-the-Pooh, originally a story book bear, the inspiration for which came from a teddy purchased by the author's wife for their son Christopher. The original Pooh is in the New York Library; this modern replica was made for a Walt Disneyworld Teddy Bear Convention by Canterbury Bears.

Opposite top: Highly stylized bears find their way onto a display plate and win awards.

Opposite below: Close-eyed companions share the same startled expression.

in England, developing an early taste for marmalade. Paddington's first illustrator was Peggy Fortnum, who gave him his shaggy appearance, together with his characteristic bush hat, duffle-coat and, ultimately, his wellington boots.

Such has been the enduring success of these characters that they have all been portrayed in television series or films, and replica teddy bears have been made of all of them from soon after they appeared. A company, Gabrielle Designs, makes Paddington Bears under licence in the UK, following the success of two that the founder, Shirley Clarkson, made for her children. Eden Toys makes them in the United States, and Christopher Robin's original Winnie-the-Pooh sits in a library in New York. In 1966 Pooh's adventures were immortalized on film by the Walt Disney

Above: Tiny Christmas teddies take their place in a festive decoration.

Opposite: Pretty in pink, this blue-eyed bear waits patiently, anxious to do only what she is told.

Company, which owns the rights to the character. Each year Disney commissions a teddy bear manufacturer to make a Winnie-the-Pooh to commemorate the Walt Disney World Teddy Bear Convention, which has been held annually in Florida since 1988. Rupert Bear teddies have been made over the years by a number of companies under licence from Express Newspapers.

Over the years all these bears have released a flood of other "bear-obilia" on the market. China, cutlery, clocks, watches, lunchbox tins, paper plates and napkins, bags and satchels, pencils and pencil cases, confectionery, clothes (and wellington boots), even talcum powder, bubblebath, soap and shampoo as well as, of course, figurines in porcelain, pottery and various other materials featuring these bears in some way, have all appeared.

A companion to 'Rumples', this is 'Buckles' who wears a very sporting pair of checked dungarees.

There is, of course, nothing new about the production of such merchandise. Teddy bear ephemera appeared as soon as the first entrepreneur recognized the success of the teddy bear at the beginning of the twentieth century. All the items mentioned above, plus a host of others ranging from teething rings to expensive jewelery, from cuff links and buttons to rucksacks, from bookends to nursery furniture, have been made in the shape of teddy bears or with teddy bears featured on them. Go to a teddy bear auction and you may well be amazed at the range of clothing and accessories featuring teddy bears in some way worn by buyers! Teddy bear manufacturers themselves have produced novelty teddies over the years, such as the Shuco miniature accessories, as well as such items as teddy bear muffs, bags, purses and hot water bottles – Steiff made one of these in the first decade of the century, the water going into a tin canister inside the bear through an opening centre seam.

Teddy bears have inspired board games and appeared on playing cards, as well as, of course, on almost every conceivable child's toy – building blocks, balls, play telephones (as well as the real thing). From the earliest times they have appeared on postcards the world over. Early examples are popular with many collectors, and collecting teddy bear postcards is of sufficient interest for the *Hugglets Teddy Bear Magazine* to have run a series of articles on this subject alone, written by Rose Wharnsby and entitled "Paws on Postcards". Many modern teddy bear manufacturers and artists produce postcards of their teddy bears today – for example, Lakeland Bears, producers of teddy bears dressed in wonderful clothes appropriate to the rugged countryside of the English Lake District, produces a series of postcards of its bears in fell and lakeside settings.

Besides being the heroes of feature films, such as the Winnie-the-Pooh films, teddy bears have famously appeared in films as supporting characters. One of the most famous in recent times was Aloysius in the British television adaptation of Evelyn Waugh's *Brideshead Revisited*. This teddy, the companion of Sebastian Flyte particularly during his time at university, actually belonged to the great arctophile Peter Bull, who had christened the 1907 Ideal bear Delicatessen because it had spent much of its life sitting in such a shop. The teddy bear's name was changed following its acting appearance, and today it is another example of a replica bear – in fact, it has been replicated both sides of the Atlantic, in America by the North American Bear Co., which brought the copyright of Aloysius, and in the UK by the prestigious manufacturer, the House of Nisbet, which called its 1987 replica Delicatessen.

If Aloysius appeared as a co-star in *Brideshead Revisited*, other teddy bears have starred in their own right. In 1995 author Moya O'Shea wrote a play for BBC Radio entitled *Theo*. This traces the fortunes of a bear from its purchase at the beginning of World War I for a young boy right up to the present when it was sold at auction. The story is compelling and, as anyone involved with teddy bears will tell you, like all bears, Theo the teddy not only has a strong and definite character, but becomes highly involved with the lives of each of its owners.

Teddy bears have been the subject of songs through the century, too. Perhaps the most famous of these is *The Teddy Bear's Picnic*, which has inspired parents to take their children on teddy bear's picnics as well as arctophiles to arrange such occasions for their most treasured bears. Teddy bears acquired this, their very own theme tune and song when Jimmy Kennedy added lyrics to the score in 1930. Since then it has appeared illustrated in countless books, and today, Merrythought plays a version of it on the company's telephone system if, for any reason, you call and are kept waiting.

A fine example of a one-off artist bear. This one is christened 'Rumples' and is 13ins (33cm) tall. His eyes are old shoe buttons and his pads are made of a linen fabric.

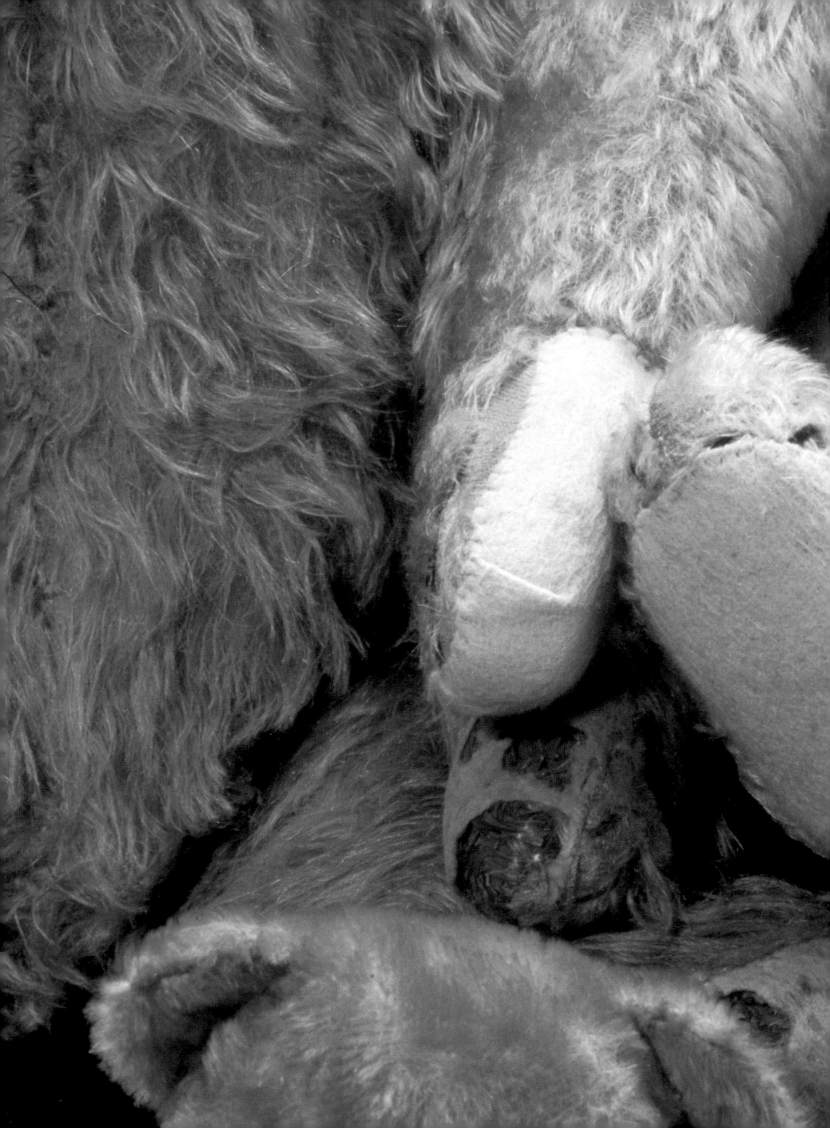

Chapter Seven
Arctophily

Arctophily

Opposite and right: A pair of highly desirable bears from a bygone era.

I t is probable that people began to amass collections of teddy bears soon after they first appeared on the market. The desire to collect lies deep within most of us, apparently related initially to the need to gather – to ingest – in order to survive. With our basic needs more readily served than they were in the days of our earliest ancestors, our collecting instinct turns towards more material things.

Collecting teddy bears today is as understandable as the fascination of wild bears was to primitive man. Their furriness makes them soft and cuddly, they are capable of standing up on their hind legs as we do, they appear to hold their arms out to us in what can be interpreted as a hugging gesture, and the fact that their eyes are set in the front of their head giving them a forward-facing expression awakens a response in us. All of these things allow us to anthropomorphize bears. Add to this the fact that most collectable teddy bears have been made by hand so that each one appears just slightly, subtly different, its expression reflecting the way that the person who stitched the face was feeling at the precise moment the bear was made. Teddy bears have become like "little people", silent, yet understanding companions, providing for many people an important link to childhood and an antidote to loneliness.

You have only to talk to people who are interested in teddy bears or to listen to the stories of those

Teddy bears read newspapers too! This jaunty chap - 'Chris the Paperboy' - was made by American artist, Mary Kaye Lee. Another bear, christened 'Lady Margaret', was created in 1991, by top American artist, Marcia Sibol, as the gossip columnist of the 'Teddy Bear Times'.

who are involved in the buying and selling of them to know that none of this is an exaggeration. Elderly people are often desperate that their loved teddy should find a new home where it will be equally treasured and cared for. The excitement of someone who has bought a bear that has caught their eye in a sale is almost tangible.

There is perhaps one man, above all, that could be termed the godfather of arctophiles, who made the collecting of teddy bears both popular and acceptable on both sides of the Atlantic. This was the British actor, Peter Bull, who collected teddy bears himself and also wrote the first book about them, *The Teddy Bear Book*, in the late 1960s. He appeared on television in the UK and USA, talking about teddy bears and doing much to promote their collection. His own particular favorite teddy was apparently a miniature Steiff dating from the late 1940s, called Theodore, which was given to

page 113

Opposite: Many early bears, such as this pensive looking creature, are now museum exhibits.

Left: Still making teddy bears, Steiff produce replica bears (of old teddy bear favourites in their former ranges) as well as bears specially for collectors. These leather-booted macho characters are all Steiff 'Nimrod Hunters'.

Left: Also by American artist, Mary Kaye Lee, this little angel, photographed in 1995, is known as 'Baxter'.

Opposite: This little bear is obviously used to a life of luxury!

Looking very traditional, this is nevertheless a modern limited edition teddy bear, called 'Samuel'. His maker was British artist, Frank Webster, who made 50 of these bears for Charnwood Bears.

him to celebrate a first night and which he referred to as "a symbol of unloneliness". Sold at Christies in December 1995, it reached £14,000 (approximately $21,000), some four times its catalogue price; its new home will be alongside Alfonzo at Teddy Bears of Witney, near Oxford.

Serious collecting probably took off in the USA first, reaching the UK in the early 1980s. From there it spread to Europe and, by the late 1980s and early 1990s, to Japan where it has grown apace. The first specialist shop, selling nothing but teddy bears and catering exclusively for the collector's market, opened its doors in the UK in 1985. Since then, the movement has exploded. *The UK Teddy Bear Guide 1996* lists over two hundred shops and sources for teddy bears, although admittedly this includes auction houses and dealers and not all the shops sell nothing but teddies. It also lists nearly four hundred bear makers and teddy bear artists who sell their bears. There are, in addition, now numbers of teddy bear

These beautiful plush bears were made by Merrythought exclusively for the collectors' market in the 1980s. All have shaven muzzles and the small bear has had the tips of his fur dyed a darker color.

Below: An artist bear dating from the early 1990s. This is 'Willoughby', made by English artist, Pam Howells, for Pamela Ann Designs. Pam Howells used to be a designer for Chiltern before she began creating her own artist bears.

fairs – some exclusively for teddy bears, others for dolls as well – at various locations in countries the world over, where manufacturers and artists will have their latest bears on sale. A collector has lots of opportunities to add to or even begin a collection.

This is still a field of collecting where it is possible to begin a collection with only a small outlay. Collectable teddies sell for as little as £20 (about $30), or you might still pick one up for even less at a jumble sale, car boot sale or charity (thrift) store. People can begin and add to a collection without breaking the bank. It attracts both men and women; even as childhood toys, teddy bears have always been "acceptable" for boys as well as girls, and the fact that people like Peter Bull and Colonel Henderson gave it their public blessing has relieved it of all possible stigma. It is constantly, it seems, attracting more people. Leyla Maniera, the teddy bear expert at Christies (which is currently the only auction house in the UK to hold one

Yet another Christmas teddy bear. This one comes with a long, fur-trimmed hat and a special wreath. Christened 'Santa', he was made by American artist, Mary Kaye Lee.

sale a year exclusively for teddy bears), says that at each sale new faces appear and every time more young people join the ranks of established collectors. The appeal of teddy bears transcends age and gender.

Anyone thinking of collecting teddy bears has much to think about however, for this is a large and wide-ranging subject. Any collection ideally needs a focus if it is to be interesting and satisfying. You could concentrate on bears from a particular period or manufacturer, or on bears of a specific colour, or on dressed bears following a particular theme – service uniforms, perhaps. You might want to acquire anniversary bears – that is, bears produced to commemorate a particular date, such as the anniversary of the manufacturer or a specific event such as Queen Elizabeth II's coronation. Mischka, for example, was the bear from the 1980 Moscow Olympic Games, while Teddy for America was produced to celebrate the five hundredth anniversary of the discovery of the New World. Your interest

Left: This bear, made by American artist Ann Inman in 1993, is creatively called 'Raspbearries and Cream'. She is filled with fragranced pellets. Increasingly in the era of artist bears, the word bear lends itself to a never-ending stream of puns!

might be in limited edition bears or it could be in bears made exclusively for different shops or organizations over the years. An interesting collection could be formed of bears used in advertising or of campaign bears, such as Smokey or Pudsey, the symbol adopted by BBC's annual Children in Need appeal. Your interest might lie in literary or other media bears; it could be bears from a particular artist or it could be what could be loosely termed "character" bears – that is, bears given a specific character by the maker, such as Humphrey Beargart, Bearly Chaplin and Amelia Bearhart, which originated with the "VIBs – Very Important Bears" designed by the North American Bear Co. A collection could centre around the bears produced for collectors' clubs, which have been established in the last few years by many of the manufacturers to offer exclusive bears to those who join the club. The possibilities are endless, and arctophiles will add many more to these suggestions.

In addition, collectors say that there may often be a sub-theme to a collection. If you were to collect literary bears, for example, you might begin to collect the ephemera that goes with these. Bear ephemera could, of course, be the main theme of a collection.

Before making any decisions about the direction of a collection, it is sensible to discover as much as possible about teddy bears. There are several books available that go into great detail about the materials that were used to make teddy bears at particular periods and by specific manufacturers. Study these and then, if at all possible, go to look at the bears in museums (many museums are devoted only to teddy bears; some to dolls as well). Viewing days at the sale-rooms of auction houses are useful opportunities to look at close quarters at a range of bears. Arctophiles say that is not enough to know that the earliest Steiff teddies had long

Above: Ready for bed, this checked teddy with her co-ordinating dressing gown is a British artist bear made by Tehidy Bears. Her label gives her the name 'Geraldine'.

Mischka, Russia's best known fairy story bear, was selected as a mascot for the 1980 Olympic Games in Moscow. Here are two of these commemorative bears.

arms, a hump at the top of their back, pointed noses and boot button eyes; you need to keep looking at them, holding them to get that indefinable "feel" about bears. And of course, you need to know when materials changed and to what.

Add to your knowledge by joining a teddy bear club – you will get membearship! – so that you can discuss your interest with other like-minded, knowledgeable souls. Teddy bear rallies and teddy bear picnics are organized by various clubs and associations in different locations. *Hugglets Teddy Bear Magazine* organizes teddy bear weekends, at which there are talks and visits to specialist shops, museums or manufacturers.

Opposite: Posing serenely for the camera, this bride waits for her bear-groom.

People will take their favourite teddies to these, and teddy bears are renowned as great ice-breakers – talking to someone about the teddy they are carrying has been the start of many a friendship.

It is also a good idea to consider whether you want to collect teddies purely out of interest and love for them – as a hobby – or whether you want to make your collection an investment, although this is likely to be most successful if it is also tinged with love. Collecting old Steiffs may still be an investment but it will also be a costly undertaking. Good limited edition teddies are likely to hold their value and will appreciate as they become rarer or unavailable. Bears with a verifiable story in their history – who they belonged to, what has happened to them – tend to have an on-going appeal, but the "verifiable" aspect of any provenance is important here. An investment in artist bears will obviously depend on how the fortunes of the artist prosper, and this is, therefore, a potentially speculative area. The era of artist bears has already seen some come and go, while others names become firmly established. New artists constantly appear and can make a name for themselves very quickly as many artists hold courses and workshops in making bears.

Where you will look for your bears will, of course, depend on what it is you decide to collect. The large

Above: 'Uncle Twiggs' was designed in January 1992 in a limited edition of thirty for the first Walt Disneyland Teddy Bear Convention. His beard is made from string mohair and his walking stick is a twig plucked from a local tree.

Left: A 1960s Steiff light tan mohair teddy bear in excellent condition - a dream for a modern arctophile.

Opposite: And here he is - dashing and debonair.

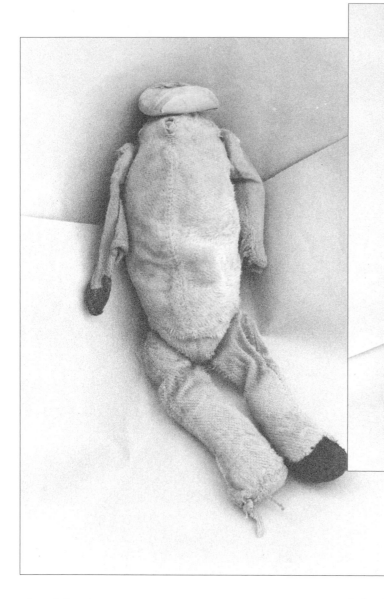

Above left and right: Before and after renovation. The bear was renovated as a 75th birthday present for the lady who had owned it as a little girl. The restorer was explicitly asked not to replace the missing paw and foot.

auction houses are good for old bears because they reach a large audience and also have experts who are usually able to recognize the maker. They will also often put a buyer in touch with a previous owner so that you can discover more about the bear's immediate past, which is always of interest to a true arctophile. Specialists shops are obviously a source for many bears. For the rest, look around junk and antique shops and other sales – but be prepared not necessarily to believe all that you are told!

Old bears in good condition will obviously command higher prices at sales than those in bad repair, but beware of bears that have been made to look old by unscrupulous salesmen – this is when you need that deeper knowledge. You can undertake repairs and restorations yourself, but again, be advised on how, or even if, you should undertake any repair by studying the magazines and books that deal with this subject. A better alternative is always to take a damaged bear to one of the excellent "teddy bear hospitals" that abound; here repair will be done by experts who know what materials to use and how to clean fur to restore it to as much health and vigour as possible.

By now you will realize that teddy bears are one of the few givers of unconditional love. This they have been doing for close on a century; it seems certain that their appeal, their friendship and their value, both emotional and material, will reach far into the next century. Remember, as one slogan runs: "A teddy is for life, not just for Christmas!"

Further Reading

Bull, Peter, *The Teddy Bear Book*, Random House, New York, 1970

Cieslik, Jürgen and Marianne, *German Doll Encyclopedia 1800–1939*,
   Hobby House Press Inc., Maryland, 1985

Coleman, Dorothy S., Elizabeth A. and Evelyn J., *The Collector's
   Encyclopedia of Dolls* (vol. 1), Crown Publishers, New York, 1968;
   Robert Hale, London, 1970

Coleman, Dorothy S., Elizabeth A. and Evelyn J., *The Collector's
   Encyclopedia of Dolls* (vol. 2), Crown Publishers, New York, 1986;
   Robert Hale, London, 1987

Hebbs, Pam, *Collecting Teddy Bears*, Collins, London, 1988

Hutchings, Margaret, *Teddy Bears and How to Make Them*,
   Dover Publications, New York, 1964

King, Constance E., *The Encyclopedia of Toys*, Crown Publishers,
   New York, 1978

King, Constance E., *Antique Toys and Dolls*, Cassell, London, 1979

Mondel, Margaret Fox, *Teddy Bears and Steiff Animals*, Collector Books,
   Kentucky, 1984

Mullins, Linda, *Teddy Bears Past & Present: A Collector's Identification Guide*,
   Hobby House Press Inc., Maryland, 1986

Schoonmaker, Patricia N., *The Collector's History of the Teddy Bear*,
   Hobby House Press Inc., Maryland, 1981

Waring, Philippa and Peter, *In Praise of Teddy Tears*, Caledonian Graphics,
   UK, 1980

Index